The Girl from Revolution Road

The Girl from Revolution Road

Ghazaleh Golbakhsh

ALLEN&UNWIN
SYDNEY•MELBOURNE•AUCKLAND•LONDON

First published in 2020

Text © Ghazaleh Golbakhsh, 2020

Allen & Unwin
Level 2, 10 College Hill, Freemans Bay
Auckland 1011, New Zealand
Phone: (64 9) 377 3800
Email: auckland@allenandunwin.com
Web: www.allenandunwin.co.nz

83 Alexander Street
Crows Nest NSW 2065, Australia
Phone: (61 2) 8425 0100

A catalogue record for this book is available from
the National Library of New Zealand.

ISBN 978 1 98854 739 8

Design by Megan van Staden
Set in Goudy Old Style
Printed and bound in Australia by Griffin Press, part of Ovato

1 3 5 7 9 10 8 6 4 2

MIX
Paper from
responsible sources
FSC® C009448
www.fsc.org

The paper in this book is FSC® certified.
FSC® promotes environmentally responsible,
socially beneficial and economically viable
management of the world's forests.

To all those who grew up in the diaspora.

May we keep telling our stories.

Contents

The Shah of Grey Lynn

T he Shah of Grey Lynn walks in front of me, his body long and lean, his head hung low. A shah is similar to a king or tsar, and Persia had been led by a shah for centuries until the 1979 revolution. We, in Persia, had legendary shahs like Cyrus the Great who wrote the world's first mandate on human rights on a clay cylinder, a copy of which sits at the United Nations headquarters in New York. We also had terrible shahs as in the last, Shah Mohammad Reza Pahlavi, who pandered to the West and believed his own hype so much that he once spent a fortune on a lavish celebration of the ancient ruins of Persepolis, the former ancient capital built up by another great shah, Darius I. But as millions in the country were poor, no one cared about the celebrations. Shah Reza Pahlavi, whose policies inspired the revolution which overthrew him, spent his final years in Egypt, in exile, much like the many citizens who would follow suit and find themselves as immigrants, exiles, refugees and asylum seekers.

The Shah of Grey Lynn wears his daily outfit like a uniform: a dishevelled blue sports jacket and light blue jeans that are two sizes too big and which hang dangerously low, sometimes dragging on the ground. To contrast this unruly look, he wears impeccably clean Allbird sneakers, the kind you see constantly popping up on your Facebook feed. The Shah has a thick head of beautiful dark hair that cascades around his head, but which stays clear of his large forehead. He has an equally thick beard that completely hides his lips, but the beard is meticulously well-kept. Buried between, lie downcast eyes. The Shah never makes eye contact, as if almost afraid to stare at the world around him. The Shah is a combination of contrasts. He is both hobo and chic; an enigma who wanders the same stretch of road in upmarket Grey Lynn day after day, slowly, without purpose and alone. The Shah does not stride, he merely shuffles, as if terrified of taking up space. I always spot him on the way to catch my daily bus, and for some reason this comforts me. Like Chicken Little, I believe that if I were to miss him one day, the sky would indeed fall.

One day I find myself sitting at a bus stop as it pours with rain; the kind of rain that comes from all directions, viciously and relentlessly. Suddenly the Shah wanders in, still with his slow pace despite the mini-typhoon. He stands under the shelter for a second, then without warning sits next to me. His eyes stay cemented to the ground.

'Should've brought my togs,' I joke then immediately regret it. Yet the Shah smiles, the first time I've seen him show his teeth, which are small and radiantly white. His face immediately melts into a warm kindness. He replies, 'I can't swim.'

I pause, wondering how to react, then he snorts a short laugh. Relieved, I laugh too. It seems that the Shah also enjoys terrible jokes.

As the rain continues its wailing, I ask the Shah some questions and he answers directly but personally. He is from a country that has battled revolution and war. He has a lot of worries. He lives alone in a tiny flat near a carpark. He hates the smell of coffee. He would love a dog. I ask him if he has any family here. The Shah grimaces.

'Sorry,' I stammer.

His face softens so I ask him to tell me the story and this is the story he tells:

The Shah grew up in a small village in a faraway land with two sisters and three brothers. They were an inseparable bunch even though his mother doted mainly on his older brother Ahmed. The Shah looked up to

Ahmed as Ahmed seemed to have it all. He was handsome and overtly kind to everyone he met. Often, the family would joke that he looked like a younger Omar Sharif. Secretly, the Shah didn't concur. Ahmed seemed much more handsome. Ahmed would consistently help people around him and his dream was to become a doctor so that he could help those most vulnerable. Their mother believed Ahmed to be too kind and that his kindness would ultimately become his downfall. The Shah disagreed. He would argue with his mother that all the greatest people valued kindness above all: the Prophet, Jesus, Buddha and probably even the great Omar Sharif.

His mother replied, 'Yes, but at what cost?'

The Shah tells me how his family's lives were seemingly normal until the Iran–Iraq war. They had the same wants and needs as most people; they desired love and acceptance and adventures; they loved good food and intelligent conversations. Yet much like my parents' situation, the universe decided to intervene with unspeakable horrors. Time suddenly stopped and a deranged timeline evolved. The universities were immediately closed so Ahmed could not continue his dream of becoming a doctor. People had to make bomb shelters out of stairways and basements. Blackouts were common so the streets were eerily empty every night. Soon the entire family except

Ahmed managed to escape to a neighbouring country, where they lived in limbo. Ahmed was left behind for reasons the Shah would not tell me. After a few years, the family moved to New Zealand as refugees, while Ahmed stayed behind in his homeland.

The war continued for years, and entire cities were almost eviscerated. Buildings that had stood for hundreds of years were mutilated. Scenes of dying citizens travelled the world and yet all the world could do was say, 'How awful!'

It was at this point that Ahmed decided to take his chances and escape. Africa was not an option. Europe was near impossible. Ahmed instead found a way to Mexico after paying his life savings to people smugglers. The Shah kept in touch with Ahmed on his tortuous journey through Mexico—a land he had never seen, with a language he had no knowledge of and a journey that could end his life at any point. It was at the border between Mexico and the United States where Ahmed was arrested. While his group ran for their lives, a woman and her infant child fell behind. Ahmed, who was always too kind for his own good, stopped to help and thus he was caught.

Ahmed now resides in Los Angeles. There are no bombs, no invading zealots, but Ahmed is a prisoner. He is an 'illegal' who has no rights to lawful work, health services or education. His dreams of becoming a doctor have been vanquished and he now works at a local burger joint downtown. The kind of place where even when you leave, the stench of the grease stays with you. The kind of place where every single employee goes by only their first name, terrified of their pasts being revealed. It is a place of forced exile, a twisted Hotel California where folks can never leave. Ahmed is forever chained to this life, for if he leaves and tries to re-enter the US, he will be arrested and deported back to his homeland. A homeland he has not seen for over thirty years.

The Shah tells me that on his daily walks he only ever thinks about Ahmed. He wonders why someone who was just being kind is now doomed to such cruelty. He wonders whether Ahmed would have been successful if he had thought only of himself. He curses the world for not reciprocating the same kindness that his brother always gave out.

I know this story. My cousin Babak lives in Greece. He has been there for almost forty years as an 'illegal', with no rights and no permission to leave. While many of us in New Zealand yearn to visit Greece for sun-soaked beaches, ancient ruins and white-domed buildings, others see it as a terrifying gateway to an unknown Europe. The route to Greece is like a demented yellow brick road and Europe indeed becomes a type of Emerald City. The utopia the

West represents is a fallacy to many who seek asylum. For the reality of being an asylum seeker is not a road paved with gold but one of fear and the unknown.

Babak was the eldest cousin on my mother's side. As the only boy he was feisty and rebellious. My mum tells me how he would always drop into her house on his way home from school for food. His first dinner, he would call it, before heading home for his second dinner. Babak, like many teenagers, had grand dreams of his future. He loved music, films and all sports. Like all good Iranian men, he was even excited about doing something prestigious but practical— law, medicine or engineering—though secretly he dreamed about becoming a rock star like his favourite singer Freddie Mercury. He once tried to grow a similar moustache, but it ended up being embarrassingly patchy. Yet Babak's fate was not his own to choose. It was chosen for him.

After the revolution in 1979, Iran was vulnerable. As internal factions attempted to group together some sort of stable leadership, outside factions were ready to pounce. Saddam Hussein was one such despot ready to exploit his neighbour for resources and power, and as such, started a war in 1980. His forces invaded through the southern borders and Iran had no choice but to retaliate. And Iran did with such brutality that the collective trauma it gathered is still fresh among the population forty years later.

At eighteen Babak was the perfect age to become a martyr and add his precious blood for the sake of the revolution. Martyrdom is synonymous with Islam but even more so with Shia Islam due to the origins of the rift between Sunnis and Shias. Unlike Sunnis who believe the line of descent from Mohammad went to his friend and advisor Abu Bakr, Shias believe the line went to Mohammad's son-in-law, Ali. Through the centuries these two factions fought until one poignant battle at Karbala where Ali's son, Hussein, bent on regaining the caliphate, was murdered. Hussein was martyred, and the legend of Shia martyrdom strengthened to almost mythological levels. In modern times, the 1979 revolution gave birth to more martyrs and the Iran–Iraq war built them up. Martyrs fight for a righteous cause, and for their ultimate sacrifice they are rewarded in the afterlife.

When the war first began, Iran was not ready. Scores of men were sent to the front line and many lives were lost. The Iranian forces were soon running out of men and so they began recruiting boys. The authorities even turned a blind eye to boys as young as thirteen taking up arms despite the official recruitment age being eighteen. Such was the case of thirteen-year-old Mohammad Hossein Fahmideh. As was customary with the true believers, he wore a large key around his neck which would allow him into heaven and he held the photograph of the Ayatollah in his pocket. Mohammad strapped explosives to his small pre-pubescent body and ran under an oncoming Iraqi tank. The Ayatollah Khomeini revered him, calling him a leader with a 'little heart'. Over a million little and big Iranian hearts died, as did hundreds of thousands of Iraqis. Thousands of others were imprisoned and many others were separated from their families and communities and forever displaced.

Babak was not one to believe in the ideologies that the state tried to enforce. Many Iranians agreed with him. My aunt worried greatly for Babak and for good reason. He received his draft papers shortly after his eighteenth birthday. While his mother wailed with worry, Babak thought how it wasn't even the worst birthday gift he had received. That accolade went to a pack of playing cards his father gave him before he left the family when Babak was five. Babak's mother and my other aunts and uncles convinced him that he had to leave. So, like hundreds of other young men who refused to sacrifice their own lives for what they saw as a pointless cause fabricated by desperate bureaucrats and religious zealots, Babak was smuggled out of Iran on a donkey and into Turkey. He stayed in Istanbul for a few days, loving the nightlife and gorgeous women, but soon he had to move on to Greece where he would board a boat for Italy. When people ask him now why he didn't stay in Turkey, Babak just shrugs his shoulders: 'I was told Europe was like Oz. The fucking dreamland.'

While somewhere like Turkey would grant Babak entry, it would never grant him the most basic of human rights such as the right to study, work or become a citizen. Many of us take our citizenship for granted, never thinking of a day when it could be stripped and the consequences that would incur. To be nationless and rootless with no rights is a distressing thought.

One night Babak and a group of young men, all of a similar age and all terrified of the journey that lay ahead, attempted to board a small rickety fishing boat in a village near Crete. They were caught by Greek authorities. Babak was arrested then released. His friends returned another night and they were successful. One of his best friends now resides in Canada. Babak refused to endure the attempt again. He never told me what had happened on that first attempt and I probably will never know. Babak now lives in Athens. He runs a local bar and sometimes he shares photos with us on Facebook. He speaks Greek with a slight accent and barely remembers his Farsi, the modern Persian language. He keeps in touch with his mother back home but he will never see her again. For Babak can never leave Greece. He has been there for nearly forty years: imprisoned against his will on a Mediterranean island, like a modern-day Napoleon.

Even today, murals of the dead from the revolution and the war line the streets of Tehran. Cemeteries are plentiful with graves and photographs of the young men who died. Some had barely hit puberty, evidenced by their scared round eyes and patchy facial hair. Every year during the holy month of Muharram, the first month of the Islamic New Year, hundreds of devotees recall the martyrdom of the young Hussein in dramatic demonstrations and parades; some even self-flagellating, crying to the heavens 'Hussein!' There are streets named after the martyrs, families have picnics alongside their graveyards and even a 'fountain of blood' stands in the middle of the largest cemetery, Behesht-e Zahra, where at one point red water flowed symbolising the blood spilt in the name of righteousness.

No one celebrates Babak and the life that he sacrificed. Like Ahmed, the grand life they imagined in the West has been cruelly stolen from them. They are prisoners in exile. Yet perhaps, like the martyrs, they too will one day achieve their gold-paved heaven. These exiled martyrs of the world.

I haven't seen the Shah for months now. It seems that as soon as I had been told his story, his duty was done and he was away again, possibly to wander another street, possibly back in Iran. I will never know.

The Legend of Seven Men and Seven Women

There is a box of photo albums that my mother keeps on the top shelf of her home on the North Shore. It's a giant box full of oddities overflowing with memories, moments and images from the past. The biggest book is also the oldest. Its edges are fraying while its cover's rich mahogany colour fades into a greyish haze. This is the album she brought from the homeland—that and her favourite kitchen knife which she still uses today, thirty-two years later. The knife miraculously still cuts, like some magical contrivance from Aladdin's magic lamp. She says she was told cutlery was expensive here.

I turn the heavy pages of the album, particularly loving the candid photos of Baby Sister whose incredible rolls of flesh and frilly hats make her irresistible to any adult. I sit with my Aunt Rose who also loves reminiscing about the past. There's something quite romantic about looking at still fragments from moments past. My aunt laughs at a particular one of Baby Sister crying in her arms, the baby's entire face red and enlarged with rage. Rose's laugh is loud and unapologetic. She turns the page and her laugh softens until there is only silence. We both stare at this particular photograph. It's a high-angle shot of the inside of a factory with a large wooden table in the centre, covered with kebabs, rice and countless other dishes, as guests ranging from adults to children mill about. The overuse of polyester and perms indicates the 1980s and sure enough I spot myself as a six-year-old at the bottom left. Dressed in fashionable dungarees and pigtails, I am the only one noticing the camera. My smile, perfected after years of practice from my amateur photographer Uncle Amir (who had moved on to solely photographing Baby Sister), looks back unknowingly. This night and possibly this moment are what would change my family's lives forever.

—

That night we all pack into our locally made Paykan cars. New foreign cars are banned. Paykans are to Iranians what the Trabant was to East Germans during the Cold War. They are badly made, constantly falling apart and have now become beacons of kitsch. The Paykan is notorious for its insane fuel consumption. But it's OK as it wastes the oil that we refuse to sell to the 'Satanic West', so driving one is brazenly patriotic. Each Paykan is packed with a family of at least five, including ours, with my parents, me, Baby Sister, Rose and her husband Amir. While an ongoing war and oppressive regime abound, seatbelts are laughable. My mum's younger sister follows with her friends in the car behind. Reminiscent of teenage summer holidays of going to the Mount, this trip also has a specific and secret purpose. Like a nomadic caravanserai we all follow one another out of the city of Tehran and make our way north to a smaller town near the Caspian Sea.

My Uncle Amir is Azeri-Iranian and so he has the best jokes. The adults always make fun of him because he is Azeri, but that's what Persians do. They also make fun of him because he's rocking a thick bushy beard that reaches up into the crown of his hair, amassed in a beautiful thick black blanket. This type of beard is encouraged by the new regime as the pious look of followers of Mohammad. Anyone who wants to get in the good books with them must don matching facial hair. Amir is an atheist, and vehemently so. He cannot even mention the regime without twisting his brow into disgust. Yet this very orthodox appearance is ruined by his piercing blue eyes. That's what made my aunt fall for him. That and his very crass and brash demeanour. Amir begins:

'A man asked a mullah, "Would you like to drink vodka or tequila?" Outraged at such an offensive question, the mullah slaps the man in the face. "What's wrong with homemade *aragh sagi* (liquor)?" the mullah asks.' The Paykan literally shakes as the adults cry with laughter. Someone even claps, clearly amused by this brilliance.

Amir only ever jokes about two things: sex and the Islamic republic, but only in secret as jokes are illegal. 'There is no humour in Islam,' Ayatollah Ruhollah Khomeini, the Supreme Leader, once said. 'There is no fun in Islam. There can be no fun and joy in whatever is serious.' My family in the Paykan begged to differ. All except me who not only fails to understand the joke but also barely knows what a mullah is. For me, women in black chadors and Ayatollah shrines pictured on my school books are the norm. I don't know a life beyond this.

Our journey takes at least four hours, not because of the distance but because Iranians love to stop by the side of the road and have tea. Not the quick and easy teabag, though, that's clearly a bastardised Western thing. No, we need our tea to be leaves only and distilled properly. The biggest and most aromatic leaves are held in the flask for at least a good ten minutes before it is poured into a clear glass (never plastic). The colour must have the right amber tone, and the correct aroma, or you have failed in your role as an Iranian, and quite possibly as a human being. Tea is taken with *ghand*, cubes of white sugar, which are clasped in the front teeth as the tea is sipped, adding a brilliant hint of sweetness—or it is mixed with a small wand of *nabat* (crystallised sugar with a hint of saffron). No milk, unless you're making fun of the British.

The group is loud, joyful and excited for their destination. Amir drops another joke. This one is not so successful and my mum tells him so. Amir replies with a curse that I love. Only later will I learn the meaning behind that word and spend years wondering why women's genitals always make the worst curses in nearly every language.

The road ahead begins to darken as evening draws near and I lose sight of our surroundings. I'm also far too enthralled in my 'art' to notice. I loved to draw and often I drew what was around me or on the TV. So it is rather shocking when years later I look through my sketchbooks and notice pages filled with protesters in chadors, soldiers on the battlefield and scores of the dead lying beneath them. My television education was an odd combination of banned Western horror films and real-life news footage of the Iran–Iraq war.

There was the time my dad and I were watching Michael Jackson's *Thriller* on a bootlegged VHS. I had never seen zombies and, from the nightmares that followed, I was clearly not ready. Yet my dad and I were cruelly interrupted by an air-raid warning. The kind most of us in New Zealand only hear in World War II films. That piercing scream that tramples your eardrums, getting louder then quieter like some annoying mosquito as you lie in bed at night. The siren loudly shrieks as images of the Ayatollah spring up on TV sets warning citizens to seek shelter. I ask my dad if we should grab sleeping Baby Sister and make our way to the basement of our apartment like we've been instructed. Bitter from years of war and angry at the regime that now dictates his life, my dad refuses. He is a dedicated cinephile and so believes that only masochists and quitters do not watch a film to the end.

'If a bomb is meant to hit us, it will hit us.'

So we sit and continue to watch the gloved one dance. This isn't the first time we've experienced an air raid, obviously. No, the first bomb to have hit Iran was a mere five minutes from our house.

Back in the packed Paykans, we finally reach our destination: a large empty warehouse where a cousin of an uncle's wife's brother-in-law works, and who lent us his key. As the cars pull onto a dirt road, the women throw off their mandatory hijabs and beige long coats. My mum fixes her hair as Rose puts on bright red lipstick, an expert at keeping her hand steady despite the bumpy ride. This is the thing about repressing even the most basic of human rights. The more something is banned, the more alluring that something becomes. In Iran, as it was then and even more so now, many women wear makeup with the precision of experienced artists and with the heaviness of a drag queen.

The party is in full swing. Alcohol is banned, of course, but so are mixed gatherings of men and women (only gender binaries are acknowledged in the Islamic Republic!). Women, men and children mill about eating vast quantities of food and the adults drink homemade vodka. Aunt Rose says that the vodka tastes like bleach and cardamom but they down it anyway. The setting has a typical factory aesthetic: cold and barren. Like having a party on a dark container ship. No one has brought a boom box so some genius thinks of blasting the tape deck from his car. He even shines his headlights into the warehouse in imitation of disco lighting. Everyone loves it as the tinny, scratchy tunes of the Bee Gees blast through. The Bee Gees are obviously banned too.

Even my mum took a sneaky sip of the vodka cardamom, my aunt says, despite nursing Baby Sister on some hardcore formula at the time. My mum wears an off-the-shoulder red top that she made herself and reveals some killer wavy locks that she sweated over getting right hours earlier. Her hijab is tossed aside as these blonde highlights need to be seen. Always fashionable, never trashy, my mum poses for Amir, but then scolds him for his angles as they will accentuate her 'big' nose. Growing up, my Kiwi friends would succumb to societal ideologies of beauty by hating their hips and butts. The 'big nose', however, is the Iranian woman's nemesis. There's a reason Iran still boasts one of the highest numbers of rhinoplasty operations in the world.

My younger Aunt Shadi, herself only twenty-five, watches from the sides with her friend, scanning the crowds for some attractive faces but feeling let down by the numerous nerds, engineers and oddballs. My aunt and her friend only date artists and writers because that's what you do at twenty-five. Her thick black brows almost meet in the middle but purposefully so, imitating those of Brooke Shields in *The Blue Lagoon*. Shadi's long dark hair cascades around her shoulders, and her gold glittery top sparkles. Her friend wears a green sequined top. Together they look like Christmas.

A much-loved Persian pop song comes on, to a roar of approval from most of the guests. Two of the more confident men create a makeshift dance floor as others join in. A woman wearing only denim dances like a Levi's goddess. Her arms are outstretched at her sides as her wrists turn delicately to the beat. Her feet step to the side and in front as she twists her hips, almost sliding around the floor. She is mesmerising to watch, and she knows it. She manoeuvres her way to some of the other guests and grabs their hands. They refuse, politely at first, but her pull becomes stronger as she literally drags them onto the dance floor to the delight of the others. Defeated, they give up and join in. Some of the less confident party-goers merely clap along, terrified that Denim Dancer will target them next.

A group of young men argue in the corner, possibly about politics, probably about football. It gets heated though, as any Persian conversation looks when viewed from a stranger's perspective. Persians love using their hands. Yet, unlike Italians, the hand gestures differ from person to person, with no consensus on meaning. One man, almost fuming, turns his hands into fists and pretends to pull out his own hair. Perhaps that's why he has the beginnings of a bald spot on the top of his head. In one photograph, my dad is next to him, merely listening, not one for dramatics or conflict. He appears to scratch his moustache a little. The thick black tuft above his lips a sense of pride for the hair he is losing above. Most of the men here sport some sort of facial hair as if foreshadowing the hipster revolution that would overtake us later. I overhear one of the men as I walk past, carefully balancing my Coke can like I'm carrying the king's sceptre. Ironically, Coca-Cola is not banned. Perhaps they made a deal with the mullahs.

'Those poor bastards in Afghanistan, they really have no choice,' the man begins.

Another jumps in, 'What about us poor bastards?'

And another, 'At least we're not starving like the Ethiopians.'

And so begins a game of figuring out who has it worse in the world right now. Even today, when I visit Iran I am amused and sometimes saddened that the consensus seems to be, 'Well, at least we ain't Saudi Arabia.'

The night continues as the homemade vodka keeps flowing and the concrete floor hosts more dancing to objectionable pop music. I lay my head down on the lap of an older woman, Khanoom (Madam) Nimtaj. She feels like my own grandmother. Her squishy body hides behind some meticulous styling. Her hair is like Jane Fonda's, complete with a faux-blonde tone and hints of a shag haircut. Iranian women do not age. Their ancestors must have made a Faustian deal with the goddess of youth.

My eyelids droop and dare to close, though I will them not to. My body wins and I drift off as I feel Khanoom Nimtaj's soft hands brush my head slowly and lovingly.

—

My memories stop there. I wonder if I have repressed that night, afraid I would lose myself for all eternity in the memory, as in *Inception*. Except there is no handsome white saviour in this story. My next memory is a vivid image of my father's back with sixty lashes oozing blood, and the wailing screams of my mother.

My Aunt Rose tells me versions of this story, which was collectively put together after that night.

Rose, rather drunk by this stage of the party, stumbles outside to the car pumping the music.

'Shut up! I have the perfect tune!' she yells, somewhat stuttering but not that pissed, or so she thinks? She fumbles in the front seat and spills some of her vodka on the leather.

'Shit,' she whispers as she tries to wipe up the evidence on the seat which has, to be honest, seen better days. My aunt fiddles with the tape deck and finally pushes play. The song begins like all Persian pop songs: a stretched-out instrumental opening, rife with a moody traditional sitar and an upbeat dombak drum until an intrusive eighties synthesised keyboard kicks off. If Persians can't dance to it, it's not real music. A soft male voice begins:

Emshab mikham mastt besham (I want to be drunk tonight).

My aunt hollers with pride as she sings along with it

and saunters back inside. Worried the vodka will inevitably run out before she's ready, she downs her cup for a refill. 'Let's get drunk on love!' she cries but stops when no one replies. The room has stopped.

Soldiers in full dark green khakis stand around the room holding their AK-47s. Some point handguns directly at the guests who seem frozen in time, not daring to make eye contact. As a soldier storms up to her, my aunt lets the empty cup drop behind her. Terrified, she looks down as the soldier motions her to go to the side of the room with the other women. They all stand in a cluster, clutching their kids or each other protectively. Someone sniffles, another shuffles her feet, but the silence is threatening.

My dad has a Colt pointed at him. I once had to ask him what a Colt was and his reaction was one of shock that a grown woman would not know basic weaponry. It's probably best not to focus on the irony that Iran's religious police, who violently resist any Western influences in their land, are still using American imported guns. Hypocrisy, after all, is an important trait of oppressive regimes.

The soldier at the other end of the Colt looks younger than my dad. A fresh beard on his face probably his pride and joy. It looks as if he's just managed to grow it past his chin for the first time in his life. He talks to his superior: a man in his thirties, sombre, with the thickest unibrow this side of Bert and Ernie. Since the birth of the Islamic Revolution, Iran has had different strands of police, with the Basij or paramilitary force being the most notorious. Some of those who climbed the ranks were uneducated and sometimes even illiterate, but with a passion to oust the imperialist upper classes and share the word of a deranged version of Islam. Some of them were just keen to get rich quickly, and in the chaos that ensued following the revolution, donning a dark robe and naming yourself a Seyed, a descendant of the Prophet, was enough to climb the ranks.

Mo, the friend of the uncle's wife's brother-in-law who gave them the key to the factory, is a local here. He whispers to my dad, 'I heard that if you eat a cucumber, it will get rid of the smell of alcohol.'

My dad is about to answer when the young soldier spots them talking. He strides over and belts my dad across the face with his hand. 'Be quiet!' he yells, reinforcing his dominance, though as my dad said later, there's no need when you are already holding a gun. Another soldier, barely looking as if he's hit puberty, runs in, his AK-47 hanging casually at his side like an old jacket. He whispers something to the superior, who finally speaks. Loudly but calmly, he proclaims that the cars are here to take them all.

'Where?' my dad asks, but the superior refuses to

answer. Everyone is led out quietly and quickly, with many staring at their shoes refusing to accept the uneasy reality they find themselves in.

My memory of the police station is loaded with Hollywood imagery. I imagined us all squished into a cell complete with large metal bars and soft-focus lighting. My mum insists that it was much more mundane. The women and children are locked in a small, sterile police room, not much bigger than an average living room. There are plastic chairs, the usual bland fluorescent lights and a small window high up in a corner which helps give the room a less dystopian vibe. Some of the women hold on to each other for support, while others sigh in frustration. Apparently, I run around wild, loving the drama. The quiet nervousness is offset by Baby Sister crying. She's awake and hungry. My mum goes full-on Mother Lion and demands the police give her access to a kettle so she can whip up some formula. Despite holding a weapon, the young policeman looks terrified and agrees quickly, running to get one. Hell hath no fury like an Iranian mother on a mission. As she feeds Baby Sister, she whispers to my Aunt Rose, 'Tell them you're pregnant.' My aunt nods, scared but still possibly a little drunk. She sits to steady herself.

The men's room projects a completely different vibe. Raucous bellows can be heard, possibly due to the drunken bodies lying about attempting to forget the severity of the situation. A heroin addict sits in a corner, his head constantly falling into a slumber then jerking up suddenly when he wakes himself with his obnoxious snoring. Another inmate, a local storekeeper, tells the men his story as he sucks on a rolled cigarette. He was having an affair with a married woman until her husband found out. He laughs out loud showing off his remaining teeth. 'She only slept with me to get some free cutlery!' The others laugh along, possibly embracing the absurdity of their situation. The storekeeper shoves the sleeping junkie, who snores louder still: 'Look at this idiot, he thinks he's sleeping at the Hilton!'

The men all laugh, some with tears rolling down their faces, possibly due to the joke, possibly not.

Early morning comes in the form of a stern middle-aged mullah. With the most sullen-looking entourage in tow, he walks in slowly, almost following his own mobile spotlight. Wearing the customary long, beige-coloured robe and bushy beard, he looks like a younger Ayatollah. Not that he'd ever admit it, but he'd enjoy the comparison for sure. With no actual experience or qualifications, the mullah is also the mayor and judge of this town. The mullah/mayor/judge motions to one of the sisters in his entourage to go to the women. This sister of the revolution wears the customary long, heavy black chador which covers her entire body making her look like a fat bat. Only her face peeks through, which allows one giant mole to protrude proudly from the middle of her forehead. Later, when I would read Roald Dahl's *The Witches*, I couldn't help but compare them to these rather dubious sisters of the revolution, giant moles and all.

The sister goes up to each of the women and barks, 'Breathe,' as she holds her face and nose eerily close to their mouths. Each woman breathes out, some trying to inhale to fool her. The superior does the same to the men. The sister purposefully misses out my nursing mother, Khanoom Nimtaj and the children. There is some mercy here but not for long. My Aunt Rose quickly blurts out that she's pregnant. The sister stares at her as my aunt blatantly twiddles with her wedding ring. After a long pause, the sister nods and moves along. The sister points at seven of the women—including Shadi and her friend, who snuffles some cries. Shadi holds herself up sternly, refusing to show emotion. Another sister steps in and takes them to another room. The police superior also points at all the men, seven in total, as the mayor/mullah/judge checks his watch, barely acknowledging it all.

'The women will be lashed here, the men will be lashed in the town centre.'

My dad tries to intercede, 'But, Sir, we are all family, you can see, there are children here.'

The mullah shrugs so casually that his very staunch demeanour disappears. 'True, but some of it just doesn't seem very, you know, Islamic,' he says, and he walks off with his entourage while playing with his prayer rosary. The women who are to be lashed are taken down the corridor as the men are led out. We are walked back into our prison cell for the rest of the day.

'Doesn't seem very Islamic' could be the mantra for the whole regime. The Islamic Republic of Iran as described by some is not really a democracy and merely a theocracy, but seems more of a 'mullah-cracy'. Some rules are based on Sharia law dating from the seventh century, others are just made up because they 'seem Islamic'. Nearly all of the rules are arbitrary. In this case, my family's crime was men and women being in a room together, drinking alcohol and listening to loud music. Dictatorships rely on oppressing their people through the most mundane ways in order to keep the fear apparent in everyday life. That's possibly why nail polish is still outlawed.

My dad later tells me how the town centre was bustling. The outdoor mosque was in the large, chaotic piazza in the middle of the town. Awash with all forms of transport known to humankind: cars, mopeds, bikes, trucks and donkey-led carts speed around the roundabout as hordes of people walk about. Many are ready for their midday prayers and loiter around the central roundabout. This day, a long, heavy bench is stationed right in the middle. The men from the party are led up to this bench as many of the worshippers stop and watch, knowing what is to occur. Others continue walking by, not at all keen to witness the barbaric show that will take place. My dad is to be the first. He wears his heavy leather jacket that he believed to look like David Hasselhoff's on *Knight Rider* and jokingly asks if he can keep it on. A guard just shakes his head until he removes it. My dad is taken to the bench and told to lie face down, but not before the lead guard apologises in advance.

'I'm sorry but I have to do this.'

My dad nods, almost softened by this token gesture of mercy. But it doesn't last. With a cable wire, the guard lashes him sixty times on his back.

The first few lashes are the most excruciating, yet the body goes into protection mode and dissociates the pain from the brain. The skin is torn in microseconds as the lashes continue and blood begins to smear the wire. Some of the crowd watches in fear, some cheer and yell 'Harder!' while many look on in disbelief. In theory, public punishments are always used to deter further 'criminal' activity. My Aunt

Shadi tells me of the days when she would accidentally walk past a public hanging. Despite not wanting to witness such an atrocity she was forced to and the experience haunts her to this day. I guess the theory works.

The guard finally finishes as he hits sixty. My dad, barely conscious by this point, is helped up by one of the guards and he seats him down by the side of the road. My dad can barely move, his body has gone into shock. The mullah/mayor exclaims to the crowd in a rather monotonous tone, 'We caught seven men and seven women defying the Republic. Fornicators and sinners, they are to be punished.'

Some of the daily worshippers cheer, believing the allegations. Others are pained to know that this torture will occur six more times. My dad tells me how in the early days many people believed such propaganda but now, decades later, it's very difficult to make the Iranian people believe such ostentatious lies. Perhaps this is why Iranians are always wary of everything and anything.

Uncle Amir is next and as one of the more sombre guards leads him to the bench, the guard fluffs Amir's beard in jest and tells the other, 'Beat this one harder.'

The other guard nods in agreement though obviously not enjoying the sadism as much. I ask my dad what the lashing sounds like, but he tells me he's forgotten. I ask him how he felt. He looks at me with that same shocked face he had when I asked about the Colt, pauses, then replies, 'It took over a month to start healing.'

The lashing continued until they reached Mo, the local. The mullah/mayor has a special treat for him. They take Mo to his business, the local panel beaters, and beat him there in front of his shop to some horrified onlookers. My dad, recalling the memory, snorts a laugh.

'His business boomed after that. He became a local celebrity.'

My memory jolts back at this point where I remember my dad rolling his shirt up to reveal his bloody wounds to us. This image is one that is cemented into my mind. That, and my mum's gasps and wails at the sight.

—

It was at this moment that Uncle Amir decided to leave Iran for good. He received a visa to one of the very few places still handing them out to Iranians: New Zealand. No one had really heard of it but as my dad says, 'They speak English and have good lamb.'

We all then make our way to the end of the world.

I ask my mum about this night that completely changed the trajectory of her life. She says, 'It's only later you learn that everyone had similar stories like that.'

The Iranians of my parents' generation have all garnered traumas from the revolution, regime and war. Their traumas are moulded into literal scars for some and internal wounds for others.

I cannot help but feel something very different to my New Zealand friends every time Anzac Day rolls around. My friends wake up early and take to the commemorative sites, or even make the pilgrimage to Gallipoli, bowing their heads and taking pride in remembering their ancestors who fought the great wars. I, too, take some pride in remembering the sacrifices my parents and their generation made for me and other Iranians in exile and the diaspora. I, too, bow my head and whisper, 'Lest we forget, the legend of the seven men and seven women.'

The
Land
of
English

When we first moved to New Zealand, I specifically remember knowing only three numbers, 'One, two, and three.' I was super proud of this knowledge, shouting it with pride as I jumped on my makeshift fort made out of couch cushions and scaring Baby Sister. I also knew 'hello', so clearly I was already so damned English. Obviously, I would be accepted with open arms.

We arrived in Auckland in 1987. It was an odd time. An old time. When everything shut on a Sunday and our television viewing was limited to only two channels. The four of us lived with Amir and Rose in a tiny granny flat in the Auckland suburb of Mt Wellington, until we found our equally tiny granny flat in the middle-class suburb of Kohimarama, with its gleaming lace curtains and mid-century floral carpets. The flat's sliding door opened to vast wild bushland, making us feel as if we were living in a permanent Kiwi bach. Not that we knew what a bach was.

Both Amir and my dad found jobs as engineers. In the multitude of immigrant stories this is not commonplace. Many times, we have met taxi drivers and kebab shop owners who had professional white-collar jobs back in the homeland. A good friend of the family completed his entire master's degree while driving a taxi in the early 1990s. He never utilised the degree, but for Iranians, higher education and its qualifications are second to none. My dad's master's in electrical engineering degree hangs proudly in a cheap brown frame in his makeshift study. It sits above his PC that still runs on Windows 97. On the other wall sits a framed 3D painting with a trout jumping out of water and almost out of frame. I always pondered as to why this 1980s relic was still on show. My dad told me that it was a gift from one of their Iranian friends when they first moved to New Zealand. After this, I never questioned the fish.

My dad had spent a few years in Southern California (alongside the many, many Iranian students of the time) before the revolution, so, unlike the rest of us, he knew enough English. While I was excited to attend school (as being a nerd requires), my mother would watch the American soap opera *Days of Our Lives* every day without fail. Decked out with her highlights and newly coiffed perm, my mother would light up her red Marlboros and switch that telly on at 1 p.m. every weekday, not because over-the-top dramatics are her thing, but because it was her way to learn English. 'The English speak too fast and the Kiwis I can't understand at all, but the Americans are slow so it's easier to understand them,' she would tell me.

Smoke free for over thirty years now, my mother sits, with her green tea, after returning home from hot yoga, as she tells me her favourite memory:

'When we moved into our first flat, there was a young family next door and they had a girl around your age, Louise. She was a lot taller than you, but so were most girls as you were a tiny thing. Skinny and really, really dark.'

That's not really the point though, Mum.

'No, but you were very dark, it was odd as none of us were that dark. Your dad and I sometimes pondered as to the science of this.'

I'm really not sure why this worried you.

'So, you were this tiny little dark-skinned, dark-haired thing and Louise was this tall, broad-shouldered, almost Norwegian giant, white girl. Together you looked like opposites. You both would play outside, running around, ignoring Baby Sister but unable to speak each other's language. She only knew English and you only knew Farsi.'

I knew one, two, three and hello.

'So, you only knew Farsi. One day I was in the kitchen and I started hearing shrieks and yells. Worried, I ran outside—'

Cigarette in hand?

My mother glares at me, so I let her continue.

'I ran outside and I saw you and Louise running around the front yard, screeching at each other, miming and grunting then laughing. You sounded like cavemen, but you understood each other. You had made up your own special language. I watched for a bit and laughed; it was something quite beautiful.'

I remember leaving Louise when we moved house. It was bittersweet but similar to when we left Iran; I was more excited than sad. Perhaps underneath it all I always knew I would be forever nomadic, destined to always keep moving, never staying put in case someone else dictated that I leave. Perhaps I wanted that sense of control, to leave when *I* wanted to leave. When we did leave our house, one of the boys from my school gave me a keepsake. It was a comic book from his prized collection. I had never read a comic book before and I don't think I ever read this one, but I recall thinking how sweet it was that he gave me a leaving present. Despite facing plenty of goodbyes, I have never been good at them—I prefer to believe that they are temporary and that people will always meet again.

Perhaps that is why I find it hard to accept final goodbyes. The excitement of leaving the old for the new is always tainted by the people we leave behind. There is a photograph of my family at Khomeini International Airport just before we boarded our plane to New Zealand. My cousins and aunts are all bawling their eyes out. I am standing proud with my blonde-haired doll, tongue out, not understanding the drama. My cousins knew it could be years before they would see us again. A whole decade in fact.

The first image I have of New Zealand is how there were small one-storey houses, no apartments, vast areas of green, and no sandbags at the primary school. I was confused at this lack of protection and wondered what backwater ghetto we had moved to. My primary school in Tehran was covered in sandbags and so to see an institution without them made me uneasy. After all, sandbags are vital in war zones. How will we protect ourselves from missiles and bombs here? Why are New Zealanders not worried about this vital piece of protective gear? Do they not have enough sand?

I also vividly remember the way in which I was ostracised and even ridiculed for not knowing English, not just by the students but also by the teachers. I attended the local primary school, a small Catholic institution near my home that I could walk to and from every day—a freedom I enjoyed as the air was fresh and the roads quiet, unlike the congested war-torn streets of Tehran that I had become accustomed to. From the beginning I was acutely aware that I was different to the other kids, not so much due to my ethnicity at this stage but more because I could not understand anything and no one could understand me. The loss of language and the inability to communicate became a daily struggle, and I was not ready to deal with this challenge.

—

I am six years old and in my first year of school. My teacher is Mrs M. She dresses like Sybil Fawlty complete with a 1960s bouffant and Elizabethan ruff. She wears the most offensive makeup even for the late 1980s—neon pink lipstick and turquoise eyeshadow or blood-red lips and purple eyeliner. She does not like the fact that I do not understand English. For our first homework assignment, I want to use my artistic skills. I think that the usual tanks and women in chadors protesting about martyrdom might be a bit too much, so I settle on drawing a house, a tree, and Mrs M and I holding hands. Typical kid drawings.

Like Picasso moving on from his blue period, I feel that my art has evolved, so it is with such pride that I take this drawing up to Mrs M's desk.

Mrs M is wearing her signature ruff, lavender pencil skirt and matching blazer, and is busy reapplying her hideous pink lipstick.

'Yes?' she asks.

'Hello,' I replied, still proud that I knew the word.

Mrs M takes the picture and looks at it. Her permanent scowl doesn't change, and she almost throws it back in my face. She yells at me something incomprehensible. The more I don't understand her, the angrier she gets. She almost screams and points to my empty chair. I leave, defeated and in tears.

At my desk, I can't help but cry. I am six after all and some strange adult has just screamed in my face for reasons unknown. Was I that bad an artist? I thought I made her look beautiful.

A boy called Ben comes and sits next to me. I didn't know much at the time, but Ben was one of the popular boys thanks to his movie-star looks. He looks scared due to my puffed-up cheeks and tiny sobs, but he decides to help me. Trying not to cry in front of such a good-looking face, I sniffle then break into hiccups. Ben smiles. The universal sign of 'it's OK'. Somehow through the miracle of mime and drawings, he helps me understand what the homework is actually about. To this day I will never forget this mini Adonis. Thank you for helping me, Ben, thank you for being the adult.

—

I am now nine years old and at another primary school. My parents have saved enough money through their tireless shift work to rent a 1960s, two-storey, two-unit house in the up-and-coming area of Northcote on Auckland's North Shore. The woman who lived there sadly died in a car crash, but as her entire family lives in Germany, the property and all its contents have been left behind. It will take them (whoever they are) a good ten years to find the next of kin. My family moves upstairs where the woman used to live and my Aunt Rose, Amir and their two sons move into the two-bedroom unit below. It's a mini Persian commune and I love it. The furniture is mid-century wood complete with leather sofas and German-language encyclopedias. Our bright red couches look almost out of place. I love playing librarian with the multitude of books on the shelves. One of the trinkets the woman left behind is a bronze bullet sculpture. I use it as a 'stamp' to check out my books. Playing make-believe came naturally to me, and even when I was alone I found ways to create my own stories and scenarios, something that has now become a useful skill for my career.

The non-Catholic school I attend is about a fifteen-minute walk away and despite Mrs M's inability to teach, I have been put up a year. I have finally learned English and I did it rapidly. I did this by reading everything and anything I could get my hands on, from serial books like the pre-teen classic *The Baby-Sitters Club* to local newspapers like *The North Shore Times*. Part of it was a need to never be embarrassed again like that day in Mrs M's class and the other part was the sheer joy I gained from reading about different worlds and characters who allowed me to escape with them even for just a few hours a day.

The Baby-Sitters Club was about a group of teenage girls in America who ran a successful babysitting business. Although they were all best friends, each friend had something uniquely different about them in order to reach as big an audience as possible. My favourite was Dawn, who was one of the newest members. After her parents' divorce, she had left her fun, surfing lifestyle in California for the cold in Connecticut. Dawn, like every other character I admired, had 'long, pale blonde hair and blue eyes' and was a vegetarian—a very big deal in the 1980s. *The Baby-Sitters Club* was so influential that a few friends and I decided to start our own club, brilliantly called The Helping Hands of Northcote. We even opened a bank account, which thoroughly amused the bank teller at the time. Our aim was to help the community through babysitting, mowing lawns and doing errands. However, no sane adult wanted to give a bunch of ten-year-olds any work and after a few months we had to abandon the club. The account stayed open.

The club was co-founded by one of my best friends, who once again looked the complete opposite to me. Blonde hair, freckles and alabaster skin, Amanda lived only ten minutes away from me and so we became inseparable. Amanda's parents were far less strict than mine and she had classic Kiwi toys that I had never encountered, such as a trampoline and the Sylvanian Families set. Amanda's birthday parties involved a bunch of rowdy kids shoving cheerio sausages and lamingtons down their throats, before heading home with tiny party bags full of garish plastic toys and candy sticks shaped like cigarettes. This was a tradition completely foreign to me. It was through Amanda and friends like her that I learned the ways of this new world, and I began to love it.

—

A new student from Albania joins our class. She's just escaped the war obliterating the former Yugoslavia. My teacher takes one look at the poor lass, who also sports darker melanin than anyone else in the class, and makes her sit with me. The girl speaks no English, so my teacher advises me to talk to her in our foreign non-English tongue. Apparently, the girl and I are not aware of this universal foreign lingua and so, after some sad attempts on my part, we both give up and sit in complete silence with her staring at me with a vicious side-eye. In later years, the girl would become one of the cool girls in school, smoking behind the bike sheds and dating older guys. Yet she always gave me that same vicious stare whenever she saw me, as if my presence would forever remind her of her foreignness.

—

I am thirteen years old and starting high school. It is a girls' school, which my parents think is best as it has a superior reputation. At the time I agreed, though years later I question the benefits of such segregation. Yes, I am less likely to be embarrassed for speaking up in a class where there are no boys, but I am also at a complete loss as to how to interact with them. I keep that one comic book in my possession, just in case. High school is daunting right from the get-go. Amanda went to another school (with boys) so I know no one. A horrifying reality for any teenager. It's also a school on the North Shore, a place that is not known for its inclusivity or diverse demographics. Back then it was like Auckland's version of Malibu but with slightly less money.

I arrive for my first day of form class wearing my freshly pressed uniform, a green tartan dress that is two sizes too big for my tiny frame. This pales in comparison with the monstrosity we have to wear for winter: a thick woollen tunic with a belt, white shirt and red tie—straight out of *Heavenly Creatures* circa 1955. If it was cold, we wore woollen tights. Ladies do not wear pants. Woollen tights, as all the girls at the school realise the hard way, scratch like crazy. Not a class went by where some poor lass did not suddenly spring up and scratch her arse in mild panic. Maybe it was a good thing there were no boys. They'd have no idea.

On this first day in form class, as is custom, I dread the roll call. It is a visceral reminder of how different you are when the teacher cannot pronounce your name or even bother trying.

Galala? Gaha? G-Haz? Giza? Godzilla? Sally?

Sometimes there's an uncomfortable silence, so I always know my name is next. Later when I finally find friends, I let the teacher squirm a little and enjoy this tiny moment of sadistic glory before yelling out my name to save them. Today is not such a day and after a few attempts of 'Gahaaa, Gahamaz,' I raise my hand. Promptly I am led out by another teacher. With no explanation, she marches me through the grounds until she asks me something and I reply. She stops, astounded.

'Oh, you speak English!'

I nod, confused.

'I was just taking you to ESL [English as a Second Language] class. We looked at the roll and saw your name and thought you'd need it, but guess not.'

And she leads me back to form class.

When I finally made friends later that year, one of them, Yoong, explained how the exact same thing happened to her. She sat in ESL class for a full fifteen minutes before realising what had happened. Another immigrant friend who attended a different high school was also made to take ESL class. Not one for academia, however, she stayed in the class for a whole term enjoying the games and easy grades, before the teacher realised she was completely fluent in English.

Yoong is Malaysian-Chinese and spent her childhood at an English school in Kuala Lumpur before immigrating to Auckland with her parents and two siblings. For her, this type of intrinsic racism was not new after enduring constant bullying at her intermediate school where once again the demographic was nearly exclusively white. Yoong had been accepted at the school as she was in the right school zone. I was not, so I had to apply and be interviewed, as did Amanda and three other girls. Despite my high grades, they all got in. They were all white and blonde, and even at twelve years old I believed this rejection was an example of racism. To this day, I wonder if I was right.

—

I am fourteen years old and enjoying high school, finally, as I have made friends who do not question my English or make fun of my name. A young family arrive from Iran and stay with us for a couple of weeks as they attempt to set up their new life in this strange land. They have two daughters who are similar ages to me and Baby Sister. All of us kids sleep in Baby Sister's and my room, where the bunk bed is now covered in blankets and sheets. Persians do not believe in sleeping bags or duvets. You need at least three heavy blankets underneath you and two more on top for ultimate comfort. These are the heavy woollen blankets that are covered in garish tiger prints or prints of tigers roaming a fictional rainforest. If your guest is not sweating profusely, then you have failed in your role as a gracious host. During those two weeks, our bedroom looked like one giant cosy cushion.

Aside from showing off my mad PC gaming skills,

with *Prince of Persia* being a clear favourite, we also take the family out to my favourite place—McDonald's. Our family doesn't really do takeaways, so going to a fast-food joint was a luxury for us kids that happened every once in a while, such as on birthdays. We go to Glenfield McDonald's, which seems to have been there for an eternity. Glenfield may be located on the North Shore but metaphorically it holds some gangster vibes. The plastic chairs and shoddy tables have indeterminate stains and the whole place wallows in a greasy mist. We love it. There's a big playground with the usual suspects—the Grimace jail, the Hamburglar bouncy thing and Ronald McDonald sitting on a bench overseeing it all like the corporate billionaire monster that he is. On this night, after we have exhausted ourselves on the germ-ridden playground, my mum calls us in. Not one to question authority, I run in, but the other girls are still playing. Their mother, Shohreh, asks me to call them so I open the door to the playground and yell their names as loud as I can: 'Nazanin! Nooshin!'

'Go home and speak fucking English,' rumbles a deep voice next to me. Two thirty-something-year-old men sitting with their burgers glare at me. My voice shrivels and I feel my whole body recoil, and all my earlier joy disappears. They continue mumbling something and then laugh. Drowning in shame, I slowly walk back to Shohreh.

'What's wrong? Where are the girls?'

I manage to stammer something to her, and she understands. Her back suddenly straightens and her face twists into something staunch. She storms over to the two men and scolds them—in her broken English. I don't remember what she actually said. In my mind, the whole scene plays out in epic slow motion with Italian operatic music over the top. The two men cower and dissolve into their chairs like melting goo. I have never forgotten this moment of heroism from this woman. Despite only having moved here two weeks prior, Shohreh knew exactly what this moment meant for me. I only wish I had her confidence in the years to come.

—

I am fifteen years old and in my favourite class—English. Which becomes ironic as the teacher, Ms B, makes a beeline for me as soon as I sit down. In her most patronising smile, she asks me very slowly, 'Have. You. Been. In. New Zealand. Long?'

I pause, smirk and reply just as slowly and condescendingly, 'Yes. Most. Of. My. Life.'

My friends next to me burst out laughing. Ms B is not impressed. Yoong has a similar experience in another class where the teacher asks her, 'Do you have a Christian name?'

To which Yoong brilliantly replies, 'It's in your alphabet, what more do you want?'

Ms B clearly took a page out of Mrs M's book, as throughout the semester she would consistently bicker about the 'Asian students' who she believed 'couldn't and didn't want to speak' English. They spoke perfect English in my opinion. The whole class began to resent her. One day one of the cooler girls, who smoked in the toilets and modelled on the side, yelled at her and called her a 'right cunt'. Another day, someone locked the door and made everyone hide beneath their desks. Ms B was once again not impressed, but this clear line of rebellion against someone so unjust always made me smile.

—

I am in my mid-twenties and back from a life-changing two-year overseas experience in London. For me, London was everything I needed at that time, and so it will always hold a special place within me. Whenever I go back, I immediately feel a sense of familiarity and comfort, despite the loud noises, masses of people and terrible coffees. I have decided to return to my studies and finish my undergraduate degree, much to my parents' relief.

One day, en route to university, I am sitting on the bus gazing aimlessly out when I hear a voice mumbling further down the aisle. I try to ignore it but the mumbling gets louder, breaking through the usual silence of the half-full bus. Suddenly I lock eyes with the person, a middle-aged man who glares at me while spouting off some vile comments.

'Oi you! Yeah you! You fucking Asians and Indians! Coming here. There should be a bomb, yeah a nuclear bomb dropped to take out the lot of ya! Fucking Indians and Asians.'

I look away, both terrified and astounded at such a blatant outburst. I do not engage, as I have learned after two years in London that you do not engage with anyone on public transport. However, the man continues, and what is worse is that every other person on the bus looks at me instead of him. They look at me and wait for a reaction. No one says anything. The bus halts at my stop and both the shouting man and I exit. I notice that he is wearing a well-pressed blue suit and carrying a briefcase. He takes one last look at me and walks off, leaving me somewhat shaken and confused.

What angered me the most about what happened that day was the way the other passengers ignored what was going on and waited for me to do something about it. I had been drawn into an abusive argument without my consent and, to make matters worse, I felt very alone and unable to confront it on my own. These days, I am thankful that more people are stepping in to help in incidents like this. A campaign by the New Zealand Human Rights Commission called 'Give Nothing to Racism' encourages people to become allies in these situations and to take direct action against racism. Being a true ally means not sitting silently and watching from the outside, but stepping in to help when you can.

—

I am now thirty-eight and still face similar experiences but I am tired of it. I am tired of people staring at me with panic in their eyes when I give them my name. I am tired of my mother being upset each time some barista fails to understand her 'accent' when she asks for soy milk. I am tired of hearing about people being overlooked for jobs because of their 'foreign' names. I am tired of the outright racism and casual microaggressions some people seem to excel in. Microaggressions are elements or small moments that are seemingly harmless but deep down are linked to intrinsic racism. Being asked where you're 'really' from. Being asked if you wear a hijab. Surprise at your English-language skills. Just the other day, I was in a cafe where a woman asked me my name and when I replied, her face scrunched up and she said, very unimpressed, 'Oh, interesting,' before she quickly made haste for the door. In academia the word 'interesting' is the worst word you can use as it is meaningless and devoid of, ironically, anything interesting.

Where Rockets Fall and Pōhutukawa Grow

n the beginning, the world was built by great kings. The noble King Jamshid was born to the legendary King Tahmure, who was known as the 'binder of demons', as he had once forced the demons of the world to reveal their secrets to him including the knowledge of reading and writing in every language. King Jamshid wanted to continue his father's legacy by guiding those from darkness to light and by destroying all that was evil. He taught humanity how to create clothing, and how to excel in their chosen professions so that no one stayed a slave to laziness. King Jamshid then ordered the demons to create clay and bricks and build superstructures like palaces. He found ways to extract precious stones from the earth and soon his palace was adorned with brilliant gems. King Jamshid's power grew like the giant trees that covered his land and before long he became the ruler of everything, except for the heavens. However, his greed demanded more so he forced the demons to build a throne made of gems and to hold it up high so that it could reach the heavens. As he sat on his throne in the sky like the almighty sun, all of the world's creatures gathered below King Jamshid and threw their gems to him. Some scattered all over the land. This was declared a 'new day' or Nowruz, which became a significant festivity to be enjoyed by all on Earth.

After three hundred years, with demons as their slaves, no creature ever died. King Jamshid's power radiated everywhere, but he made a fatal mistake by believing in his own power and denying the true power from above.

———

The hilltop is crowded with people and worshippers milling about together, enjoying the warm spring. Tiny lights are wrapped around the wild trees and on the few, small clay buildings. A family of young sisters walk past dressed in traditional Iranian Kurdish dress: sparkling dress over loose pants that are cinched in at the ankles. One wears a long silk waistcoat covered in colourful sequins; it makes a loud swish as she walks. Persian carpets cover the brick ground as seated families eat their home-cooked meals, content with the fading dusk. The Zoroastrian temple is heaving with life.

When I visited Iran in 2010, I met up with a cousin of my friend Shirin's, Homa, who was an avid traveller. She invited me to join her and her friend Hamid on a three-day trip to the north-west of Iran, the region of Kurdistan, which is close to the Iraqi border. The Kurds are one of the indigenous peoples of what used to be known as Mesopotamia. They now have no country to call their own after decades of persecution, and so mainly live in the region that roughly encompasses western Iran, northern Iraq, south-eastern Turkey and northern Syria. Kurdish fighters, including a prominent number of women soldiers, became the most important allies in the fight against ISIS in Syria, after its devastating civil war.

At the hilltop, we visit one of the religious temples where images of Zarathustra/Zoroaster (the prophet who created Zoroastrianism) are laid out on a large white table in the centre, as barefoot worshippers walk around him, asking for blessings and even kissing the sides of the tapestries. The temple is covered in colourful tapestries and carpets, filling the room with warmth. Each worshipper walks out with their back to the door because it's disrespectful to turn your back on a prophet. Zoroastrianism is one of the world's oldest religions, the first monotheistic faith and the first to include notions of heaven, hell and free will.

The biggest celebration in Iran is Nowruz/نوروز, which

marks the beginning of spring in the northern hemisphere and the new year. It falls around 21 March of every year; the date depends on the exact moment the sun crosses the equator. Nowruz has its roots in Zoroastrianism as well as in Iranian myth. One of the most revered texts in Iran is Abul-Qâsem Ferdowsi's ancient epic poem *Shahnameh: The Book of Kings*. Ferdowsi narrates the early days of the world and the days of the Persian Empire, blending mythological and supernatural beings into the stories. Similar to Christian biblical stories, the chapters in *Shahnameh* reflect the eternal battle between good and evil. In the story about King Jamshid, the origins of Nowruz are explained.

Nowruz is about renewal, which is symbolised by heralding in the spring. For two weeks everything in Iran closes as people visit family and friends, and celebrate the incoming new year. It has similarities to the Lunar Chinese New Year where adults give children presents, often money, and families take special meals together. Despite the introduction of Islam in the seventh century and even after the 1979 regime change, Nowruz proved too popular to disband, and so like Zoroastrianism it has blended into a mix of traditional Iranian culture with that of Islam. Different ethno-religious peoples celebrate Nowruz as well, from Iran and Afghanistan to the Caucasus and South Asia. In 2010, the United Nations officially recognised the

International Day of Nowruz. We are proud and sometimes amused when Western world leaders take a moment to wish everyone 'Nowruz Mobarak', with President Obama nailing the best Farsi. Trump became the first president in a long time to not broadcast a Nowruz address.

A special Nowruz table spread, the *Haft-sin*, is created in every household for the week. The *Haft-sin*/هفت‌سین must have seven symbolic foods that begin with the Farsi letter *sin*/س, ranging from universally known things like an apple/سیب and garlic/سیر to more Iranian-specific foods such as the sumac spice/سماق and sabze/سبزه (sprouts grown in a dish symbolising grass and growth). Often there are painted eggs, a mirror, goldfish and a significant book of wisdom. Some people place a Koran while others opt for a book by the revered ancient poet Hafez/حافظ.

One of my favourite traditions is to get my fortune told by Hafez. A person thinks of a particular problem they are currently dealing with, flips the pages of a Hafez book and chooses a random page. The poem is then read aloud and the symbolic meaning taken is supposed to answer your problem and recite your fate. My Aunt Rose loves doing this with me, and together we spend hours attempting to deconstruct the poem we have randomly landed on, often ending up more confused than when we started.

Persians are near obsessed with fortune telling. We will find any way and any object that can be used to determine our fate, from ordinary playing cards to Turkish coffee. No matter how rational or scientifically minded a person is, there is no escaping the mysticism that has become intertwined with our culture. When I visited Iran, my cousin Naz insisted I visit her very own psychic. The psychic was reluctant, doing this only as a favour to my cousin. She was tired of telling fortunes and even her husband warned her that it was not a 'respectable' vocation for a woman.

We met in the psychic's small basement room that was enclosed in gleaming white tiles. A plain table sat in front of a half-full bookshelf. It felt like being inside a high-school dean's sterile office. The psychic was a woman in her fifties, with no distinguishing features except her very dark, almost black, head of hair. She wore ordinary clothes and had only a few pieces of paper in front of her and a simple blue pen. But there was something implicitly different in the air. It was dead silent and the woman almost looked pained to be doing this.

The psychic began in such difficult Farsi that Naz had to translate for me as we both vigorously took notes. The psychic was scribbling continuously as a jinn stood nearby, telling her about my fortunes. Only she could hear the jinn. The longer the jinn and psychic conversed, the eerier the meeting became.

The jinn is a cultural figure in Persian mythology and is at times combined with Islamic folklore. Unlike the more well-known genies who are subservient figures, the jinn has free will and so can be an antagonising force. Similar to Islamic cosmology, the world is split into the 'seen' and 'unseen', the latter of which harbours angels and demons. The jinn lives in an in-between place but can see both the seen and unseen worlds. As the jinn has free will, it has the choice to become 'good' or to become an 'evil' devil/شیطان.

This 'in-between' seems to be the definitive place for those forced into exile as well as for those growing up within two cultures. As a child, like so many other immigrant children, I tried very hard to reject my Iranian roots and declare myself Pākehā. (The world I inhabited at that time was dominated by Pākehā norms and values, without much thought given to Māoritanga/Māori culture.) I was embarrassed of my name, my look and how my parents had 'accents'. Yet thankfully I did not completely forsake my Iranian heritage, and as a teenager I returned to loving it *because* it set me apart from my peers. It was finally 'cool' to be different. It helped that I was a drama geek and into the arts, where marginalisation is often celebrated rather than feared.

Soon that in-betweenness faded as I began to accept myself as a hyphenated identity. I would now declare myself to be both an Iranian and a New Zealander. The power of being a hyphenate is that I do not have to be only one or the other, and both are celebrated equally.

In *All Who Live on Islands*, Rose Lu writes about her own memories of growing up as a Chinese immigrant in New Zealand. She also believes that her cultural identity is no longer in-between but 'as a symbiotic relationship, two twinned vines growing up in tandem'. It makes for a hopeful image.

I am also different to the Iranians who grew up in Iran and even the Iranians who grew up elsewhere in the diaspora. A part of me will always be jealous of my cousins who grew up in North America, among the larger diaspora. While it was often a rarity to find another Iranian in New Zealand, or to explain what Iran was to some curious Kiwis, my cousins have had direct access to their Iranian heritage through the many Iranians that make up their communities. As a result, they speak better Farsi because they hear it around them; they have more Iranian friends, often marry into Iranian families; and most importantly, can visit the multitude of Iranian restaurants and stores so as to keep that vital culinary link to the homeland alive.

A decade later when I look back at my notes from that day at the psychic's house, translated by Naz, I ponder at the things that surprisingly came true. Some were so detailed, such as predicting that I would spend only ten months in LA. Some never occurred, such as the love affair with the handsome stranger with a scar across his forehead (she may have been a big Harry Potter fan). But this fascination with the occult is something I will always hold an interest in despite the more logical, rational side of my mind constantly attempting to disprove it.

There are so many traditions that have accumulated over the centuries in Iran that it becomes difficult to establish their origins. Added to my own mix are traditions from Pākehā and Māori cultures that contributed to my confusion while growing up. I love the fact that I can enjoy more than one new year and often celebrate four: alongside the Western New Year on 1 January, there is our Iranian New Year in March, Chinese Lunar New Year and the Māori New Year, Matariki. A Brazilian friend, Leandro, once told me that it was traditional in Brazil to buy new underwear for the New Year based on colour, as each colour symbolises the fortune for the year ahead, such as yellow for financial prosperity or pink for love. Over the last eight years, I have been buying red or pink underwear and wearing it on the four different new years to give myself four extra chances. The undies have yet to deliver.

The last Wednesday before Nowruz begins is Chaharshanbe Suri/چهارشنبه سوری, which also has origins in ancient Iranian customs when people jump over three burning fires as a way to exorcise any sickness or negativity from within. In Iran, it is quite normal to see people jumping over open fires. In New Zealand, not so much. Our first attempt to build a small fire in our New Zealand backyard was greeted with a stern visit from council officials and a modest fine. In later years, we jokingly would play a fire app which showed a lifelike fire and we would jump over the phone. Some traditions are too important to let die.

The end of Nowruz is called Sizdah Bedar/سیزده بدر and involves families and friends going outside for picnics and throwing away the sabze (sprouts) into running water to signify throwing away the negativity the sabze had collected from the home over the last two weeks. Iranians adore gardens and picnics. In Iran, the garden has been significant as a place of paradise since the days of the Achaemenid Empire; in fact the word 'paradise' is taken from the ancient Persian word *pairidaeza*, meaning 'walled garden' or 'orchard'. Gardens in Iran are seen as safe, comfortable, heavenly and paradise-like; it's where one sits and contemplates and philosophises. Parks in Iran are well-kept and often frequented by families, especially in the evening when the temperature is cooler. Picnics become big affairs with extended family and friends gathered to sit on heavy blankets, eating from a feast they slaved over for days before. It is not merely a sandwich and wine, but dishes of rice, stew with lamb or fish, spices, and side dishes of yoghurt, fresh herbs and flat bread.

It is an incredible feat to keep traditional customs alive when living in a place where hardly anyone else shares knowledge of these customs. My parents remained friends with the few Iranians they met when we first moved here, and together they became a surrogate extended family. In the early years, when my parents could be bothered, we would organise Nowruz parties, often at a small town hall or restaurant, much to the delight of the other diners. Often they looked on in astonishment at the glitz and glamour these groups of people brought with them. Persians do not do things by halves. There is no casual dress for an Iranian: it is sweatpants and slippers at home or a ball gown and heels when out. Women would spend the few days before an occasion buying the perfect dress and having their hair done, and acknowledge it all by taking a million and one photographs at the event, much to the dismay of their children. When I moved to London for the first time, my mother's advice to me was, 'Find an excellent hairdresser and tell no one about them. You don't want any other Iranians swarming to your find.'

One Nowruz was held in a small seafood restaurant where the last diners were a group of four Pākehā seniors. Curious, they stayed on, captivated by the Iranians who love nothing more than to boast about their traditions and culture to anyone willing to listen. The seniors seemed to enjoy themselves as they ate the never-ending food and they even danced, imitating what they could from the confident dancers. Each family that attended has photos of those four seniors, with their arms in the air, smiling ear to ear. This guest culture is serious business in the Iranian psyche. Guests are always put first, as your treatment of them is a reflection of you. If a guest stays at your home, you will undertake whatever is necessary to make them feel at ease and comfortable, especially if they are older. Numerous times I have slept on a living-room floor, smooshed in between heavy blankets and the limbs of various cousins, so that our adult relatives could have our beds. It is all about sharing and community.

The first week my mum worked at Māori Television, she came home beaming as the station would share food at lunch. 'Just like us!' she would say, so ecstatic to be able to enjoy such an important shared custom. However, it was quite a shock when at primary school, for a shared lunch, we were asked to bring a plate. I remember standing for twenty minutes with my parents attempting to understand what they meant by the word 'plate'. Still unsure, my mum quickly whipped up some Salade Olivier (Russian Potato Salad) for me to take and place among the numerous packets of crisps and Tim Tams—much to my relief the next day when I realised that it simply meant shared food.

My friend Yoong was not so lucky. Asked to bring a plate to her school's lunch, her mother angrily asked, 'What kind of cheap school is this that they don't have basic service wear?'

Yoong was forced to take an actual plate and endure the humiliation from her peers.

Our Sizdah Bedar in the early years often took place at Cornwall Park near One Tree Hill, a large, well-manicured park in the middle of Auckland city, full of giant trees and green spaces. The families would gather en masse under the bright red flowers of the pōhutukawa trees and take over an entire section of the park, much to the amusement of couples out walking their dogs or lone joggers zigzagging their way through our crowd of parents, kids and hangers-on. One year, my favourite teacher from school, Miss Wood, was attending as she was dating an Iranian man. I felt so proud to have my very own guest that I could show off to all the other Iranians. My mum made sure I wore my best overalls and styled my hair in the tightest pigtails. Sitting side by side with Miss Wood, I would proudly explain to her the various foods and how to eat them like a real Persian, using a fork to collect rice onto a spoon before eating it along with a small handful of herbs. Miss Wood was curious to learn and loved my passion for teaching her.

There is a reason most people learn new cultures through food. It is a shared, communal love affair where each dish holds mysteries and histories. Afterwards, it is custom in Iran to tape the sabze to the bonnet of cars before driving to the place where it's thrown away. Every year my mum and dad, in secret, would take the sabze to a nearby walking track and throw it into a creek with the hope that the sprouts were taking away all the ills and negativity of the year.

In Iran, Zoroastrianism was not completely obliterated but merely blended in with Shia Islam and the new regime. Above the gates to the temple I visited stands a photo of Ali, the Shia Muslim martyr. Other cultures, peoples and most faiths are accepted in Iran but they will always be secondary to the one 'true' faith that the regime dictates. This shouldn't come as a surprise because, after all, we only widely celebrate Christian holidays in New Zealand, despite the land having been founded by tangata whenua. Christianity seems to be the one 'true' faith.

When I was in primary school, we had voluntary Bible classes. I was curious to attend as it meant time out from other classes, like home economics, which I despised, mainly because the food we were forced to make seemed to come from British wartime rationing. I adored more exciting classes where dangerous equipment could take your finger off, like woodwork. The wooden tray I made in my second year at intermediate is still used by my mum to hold kebab skewers before they're thrown on to the barbecue—which, thinking about it now, perfectly represents the ultimate blend of Iranian and New Zealand cuisines.

My dad encouraged me to attend the Bible classes as he believed it important to learn about other faiths. After all, there was already a Christian bias in my other classes. Choir rehearsal often centred on singing Christian hymns, our school plays would always involve the nativity story, classical literature often referenced biblical stories and many a time I was invited to attend a church service with Christian friends. However, in my quest to learn more I began to muddle everything up. For the longest time, I thoroughly believed that Adam was the first ape to have stood up.

I was so obsessed with learning more about New

Zealand and the West that I stayed completely ignorant of my own culture and anything related to the East. School did not help. Our classics education focused only on ancient Greece and Rome. The languages we could learn seemed outdated, with slim choices between French, German, Japanese and Latin.

For years, I grappled with the word revolution/انقلاب. I would hear my parents discuss it and knew it incited pain. I believed it to have been a bad word, possibly connected to war and destruction, which is not exactly true. It was not until my final year in high school that my history teacher insisted I learn more about my home country.

Mrs Atkinson was one of those teachers who seemed to love everyone. She was quiet and confident with the patience of someone who had been teaching for decades, but had not let it destroy her spirit. She was quite short with a brilliant head of curls that made her look like a modern-day Janet Frame. For our final-year research project, we could pick any historical event or person to focus on. I inexplicably chose Abraham Lincoln. Mrs Atkinson rolled her eyes and sighed, 'Ghazaleh, why don't you do something from Iran? Like the revolution?'

I was gobsmacked. How did she know about this word?

Mrs Atkinson sadly passed away in 2019 but not before making historians out of so many of us.

The Iranian Revolution of 1979 was, like many revolutions, the result of widespread discontent among all classes of people and the involvement of foreign powers over many centuries. Persia under a monarch was at one time the largest empire on Earth, surpassing Greece and Rome. Only in the twentieth century did Persia become Iran, which is the original name given to the area of Fars where the Aryan peoples lived before moving on to what is now northern India. Iran was always a strategic position for European powers, in particular the UK and Russia, both of which were heavily involved with trade (namely oil) and territory under the Qajar dynasty (1794-1925). It is not surprising that their influence and interference would create problems in the twentieth century when moderate prime minister Mosaddegh attempted to nationalise Iran's oil. Infamously remembered for the involvement of the CIA, there was a coup in 1953 in which Mosaddegh was overthrown and the Shah of Iran regained complete control. The Shah, Reza Pahlavi, was the first-born son of Reza Khan (who renamed himself Reza Shah), a general who had declared himself king after overthrowing the Qajars in 1925. Reza Shah made huge efforts to modernise the country by imposing strict changes to all aspects of traditional life, including lessening the power of the clerics. Progressive changes to the economy, judicial system and military were made to 'Westernise' the country, whereby Reza Shah began to monopolise decisions. The often oppressive measures on religion were continued under his son Mohammad Reza Pahlavi, who secularised co-education and made budget cuts, so many *ulama* (Islamic scholars) could not teach. Many in opposition were arrested or exiled, such as the Ayatollah Khomeini, who fled to Iraq and then France, from where he sent messages back to his followers in Iran. Reza Shah's rule became autocratic and included the involvement of the notorious secret police SAVAK, modelled on Israel's Mossad. Any political opposition was quickly silenced by imprisonment, banishment or even death.

My parents worked at the state national television station where they first met. My dad tells me how, during the most tumultuous time under the Shah, it was not uncommon for colleagues or even friends to suddenly 'disappear'. One time, he had seen some anti-Shah graffiti carelessly drawn on the bathroom stalls at his work. The next day, one of his colleagues went missing and was never heard from again. Another friend tells me about his uncle who was arrested many times for his Marxist beliefs. His uncle had to escape prison and spent months alone in the countryside before fleeing to the UK. Today, many secular

Iranians seem to forget the oppression of the Shah, mainly due to the horrors of the regime that followed.

The Shah was consistently backed by outside powers, including the UK and US, so much so that he was seen as a 'puppet Shah'. Soon protests began with simple open letters, which turned to national strikes, protests and even militancy from guerrilla groups. It was remarkable that opposition to the Shah came from nearly every group in the country. Many joined in the resistance to the Shah, from the secular urban left, Marxists and guerrilla fighters to religious leaders, rural workers and farmers. On 16 January 1979, the Shah departed, leaving behind a new premier. Khomeini returned to a huge welcome on 1 February, and ten days later a new coalition was made between the premier and Khomeini. On 22 September 1980, noting the vulnerability of Iran and its own need to suppress similar uprisings in its own country, Iraq declared war on Iran.

—

The very first bomb dropped on Iran was in the capital Tehran, just minutes from our house. Many people believed Iraq would attack the airports and other important landmarks first. Our house was a good forty-five minutes away from the airport and so it was with much shock and confusion that we awoke the next day to desperate friends and family calling to see if we had survived.

Loud, piercing air-raid sirens would warn citizens to seek shelter. Most people in Tehran lived in apartments so we would join our terrified neighbours in apartment basements and nervously wait out the night. I have limited memories of these nights, much of them mixed with images and scenes from films or books written about the war, or from stories told by friends and family. The screeching sirens and the photograph of Khomeini beaming from the television set directing citizens to take cover is forever imprinted in my mind and immediately triggers an internal discomfort whenever I hear something similar in films.

Alongside sandbags and basements, the only other protection we had was using masking tape on windows to hold them in place as the earth would tremble each time a bomb hit. Bombs are terrifying enough, but once Iraq began launching missiles, a new horror emerged. Missiles came directly from Iraq and often attacked without warning, as there were no airplanes to indicate their arrival. The sensation was similar to standing on tarmac and becoming overwhelmed with the intense noise of an airplane landing. The sound a missile makes can pierce you like a blade, as well as completely destroy an entire neighbourhood. There is no surviving a missile attack. The war continued for eight years; we left halfway through, but the majority of my extended family on both sides were forced to stay and endure.

My Aunt Shideh from my dad's side was a school teacher. She was the second oldest out of six children. Shideh married young, to an officer in the Shah's military who later became a military prosecutor then a judge. They had met through a cousin and my grandfather refused to let her marry until she had finished her studies. When the regime was ousted after the 1979 revolution, her husband was forced to retire.

Shideh worked as a teacher at a local girls' high school. She loved teaching and her students provided her much comfort in such a dire time. The schools stayed open for a while during the war to keep morale high and help provide some sense of normality after so much upheaval.

One morning when Shideh is at school, she stops to look around at the untouched sandbags against the buildings and notices the way students quickly scamper to their classes, afraid to stay outside.

Suddenly, the vice-principal appears and grabs her arm, and Shideh jumps in fright, as is her usual way. Shideh is not one for surprises—her high-pitched shriek can often be heard when anyone or anything appears unexpectedly within her periphery.

'Shideh, we need to talk,' says the vice-principal, her usually stern voice trembling a little.

Shideh walks with her to the principal's office.

Inside the women sit, each wearing their matching navy hijabs and coats; Shideh's hair complete with honey highlights slightly peeking through.

The principal, an elderly woman who still applies mascara despite the ban on makeup, looks directly at her desk, afraid to lock eyes with anyone. She opens her mouth, sighs and then pushes through. 'Shideh, your student Tanaz. She was killed last night—'

Shideh cries out loud, 'Oh God! Oh God . . .'

The principal continues but Shideh can't listen. Her head is filled with images of this girl from only yesterday. This girl who smiled at Shideh when she said goodbye. This girl who told Shideh that she would miss her as her family was leaving Tehran for the countryside to be safe. This same girl who told Shideh that she would keep at her studies for her wish was to be accepted into university.

In a cruel twist of fate, the girl was in a car with her family leaving Tehran. They were intending to escape to safety when a bomb fell onto their car, immediately killing the entire family.

Later, Shideh goes to her classroom and looks to the empty seat where Tanaz used to sit. A small bouquet of white lilies has been placed on her table. Even forty years later, this image stays with her.

—

Iraqi dictator Saddam Hussein, noting the vulnerability of Iran after the revolution, decided to invade in 1980, though Iran was soon on the offensive. The war lasted for eight years, and involved the mandatory drafting of men as soldiers, alongside volunteers. Numbers of those killed and wounded vary greatly, with one estimate stating that 500,000 Iranians were killed with one million wounded. Another estimates one million Iranians killed alongside 250,000 to 500,000 Iraqis. Many Iranians left during and after the war, fleeing to Europe or North America.

The regime change after 1979 was also a factor for the mass exodus. Strict religious laws were forced on the population, with many punishments harking back to archaic Sharia laws such as public lashings and hangings. Soon, due to the regime change and the war, sanctions were imposed and most countries in the West shut their borders, with the result that many Iranians attempted illegal crossings into Europe or elsewhere.

As in most wars, resources become scarce, so it quickly became common to see day-long queues for gas, bread and other necessities. The economy had so completely broken down that it became more profitable for Iranians to buy foreign currency and exchange it back to Iranian rial. A popular tactic, for those who could manage it, was to go on holiday to a country that still allowed Iranian visitors, such as Turkey or Greece, buy foreign money from the bank (proving that you were going overseas), then exchange the money for a higher return. Partly because of this and partly because of the need to take a break from the chaos surrounding us, we took a holiday to Greece in 1985. Our photographs reflect a typical family vacation: the three of us on the top of a hill looking down on the Acropolis and lazy sunny days on the beach, suntanning in swimsuits, completely able to forget the utter devastation and oppression happening back in Iran. Many Iranians also used these opportunities to visit foreign embassies that no longer existed in Iran to seek exit visas.

I ask my dad whether they did that in Greece. 'I went to the US embassy but the line was way too long and I couldn't be bothered waiting.'

Perhaps they believed that the chaos was only temporary. That things would return to the normal they knew before. The year 2019 marked the fortieth year since the revolution and proved that the Iran they knew never returned.

—

My Aunt Shadi is the youngest of six on my mum's side. As her older sisters and brother married and moved out, Shadi began studying for her university entrance exams. A studious pupil, Shadi was ecstatic to learn that her high grades would mean immediate admission. However, for Shadi and for so many young Iranians during this time, the regime change and war would harshly interfere with any plans or dreams they held. One of the first acts a regime undertakes in order to gain control is the closing of institutions like universities for fear of protests and upheavals from students, who are likely the first groups to rebel. When the Shah was ousted during the revolution, his departure further deepened Iranian people's distrust of foreign powers, particularly the US. Despite their own insistence on the importance of human rights, the US never interfered with the Shah's oppression or denial of human rights in Iran. During the revolution the US refused to support him and was even involved with the opposition, yet when the Shah went into exile, he was allowed into the US for cancer treatment. This prompted a group of students to take the US embassy in Tehran hostage for 444 days, demanding the US return the Shah to face trial in his homeland. The hostage crisis prompted the US to deny further entry to the Shah. He fled to Egypt where he died from complications from cancer in 1980.

The hostage crisis was a constant fixture on US television, prompting anti-Iranian protests and xenophobia among the country to such an extent that some Iranians in the US would declare themselves Jordanian or Lebanese. In Iran, the crisis barely got a mention; as my parents note, 'We had other shit going on.'

Shadi never got the chance to attend university as they were closed during the war. Instead, she worked in administration in various offices. Her resentment towards the regime and the era in which she lived never fully subsided. She would tell me terrible stories of what life was like in those early days when the regime was at its harshest and the war at its deadliest.

A good friend of Shadi's was cooking when a bomb dropped on their apartment block. Her father, who was in the lounge, died instantly, leaving Shadi's friend in the kitchen completely unscathed.

The Komiteh was the most feared police group during that time. They had their own female enforcers that roamed the streets dictating 'morality' to women across Iran. They wore loose black chadors and waddled in groups, their faces starkly naked of any makeup and their eyes focused on their own sense of self-righteousness. Some women called them 'penguins'. Shadi tells me how they would stop women on the street and bark at them to pull their hijabs right or remove their makeup on the spot. There were awful rumours that some of the more vicious penguins would hand over tissues that hid tiny sharp pins so that when a willing woman wiped her eyes, she would pierce and possibly blind herself. Shadi always took her own tissues and insisted she wipe her own makeup off whenever confronted by these Penguins of the Republic.

—

No one knows the exact number of people living in the Iranian diaspora. One reason could be due to the way Iranians identify themselves. A nation as large and as old as Iran has a diverse population, based in differing ethnicity, religion and language, so there can be a reluctance for people to identify as purely *Iranian*. A long list could include Persian, Baluches, Lurs, Gilakis, Mazandaranis, Kurds, Talishis, Gabrs, Laris, Laks, Semnanis, Gurans, Azeris, Brahuis, Qashqais, Turkmens, Arabs, Armenians, Kalimis, Asuris and Hazaras. These groups speak numerous languages such as Farsi, Kurdish, Arabic, and have religious affiliations that include, but are not limited to, Islam, Judaism, Christianity, Hinduism and Zoroastrianism.

The word 'ethnicity' is complex and is dependent on which discipline it is used in. For example, the New Zealand census has historically lumped Iranians under the highly varied MELAA section, which encompasses the entirety of the regions of the Middle East and Latin America *and* the continent of Africa. According to Statistics New Zealand, in 2018 this group made up only 1.5 per cent of the population.

The highest numbers of Iranians in the diaspora live in the US, with the majority located in Southern California. Many scholars believe the reason is to do with the types of immigration that occurred just prior to and after the revolution. Prior to the revolution, many middle- and elite-class Iranians were sent to study at universities in the West, particularly in the US. My dad spent his undergraduate years at a small college in the Napa Valley, California. He grew an impressive (culturally appreciative) afro, worked countless hours at a restaurant and bar to make ends meet, and was one time held at gunpoint by police who thought he was a criminal. My Aunt Shideh told me how living in the US changed my dad from a boy who used to constantly pick fights with everyone to a man who believed in gender equality and loved listening to Pink Floyd. So, in the days leading up to the revolution and just after, many people immigrated to where their sons and daughters were studying, often in large cities that provided economic opportunities for work, like Los Angeles. My dad, however, had returned early with no idea of the forthcoming revolution. He would leave Iran again exactly a decade later.

When I lived in London, I used to frequent an Iranian shop in the leafy suburb of Ealing. Like most Iranian stores in the diaspora, it was packed to the brim with nuts, spices, dried herbs and canned goods from the homeland, plus fresh cakes and pastries. Not a single space was left untouched—even the walls were plastered with Persian miniature paintings and posters of forthcoming shows of exiled Iranian singers. The shops were always open and used every kind of light ever known, from fairy lights to fluorescent, each with the aim of beaming out beyond the neighbourhood like a tiny lighthouse beckoning in its community. Nearly every day I would venture into one particular shop and ask for a single roulette cake. These are French-inspired patisseries of baked Swiss rolls spread with saffron-infused fresh cream. Most people would buy these in boxes of five to take as gifts when visiting others at their home. I would devour each roulette at the counter, like a fanatic taking their latest hit.

Every couple of weeks I would go to one of the many Iranian restaurants and order my favourite meals, which only my mum or aunts knew how to make back home. It was glorious to me because these little bastions of Persian cuisine and nuggets of Iran do not exist in New Zealand.

In Auckland, there has been a constant flow of Iranian restaurants: one will open, much to the delight of the tiny community, but it cannot sustain itself and so closes, and then another emerges from its ashes.

In contrast, hundreds, then thousands, of Iranians made Los Angeles—the epicentre of the Iranian diaspora—their home before and after the revolution, with the majority of Iranians living in the very affluent Beverly Hills or Orange County. When I lived there, near the impoverished (but soon to be gentrified) downtown, I would take a two-hour bus ride to Westwood where various Iranian businesses lined the main boulevard. There were music shops selling only Persian music and speciality ice-cream shops selling products that were drenched in saffron and rose water. I found a hairdresser who would gossip and chat as she would dye my hair, often badly as she was not trained. She became a hairdresser when she moved to LA as her credentials as an architect were not accepted. This area even became officially recognised as Tehrangeles—a portmanteau of Tehran and Los Angeles—on Google Maps.

I loved that these shops had signs in Farsi and that American friends would tell me how they would learn some Farsi as most of their customers were Iranian. Beverly Hills even had an Iranian mayor at one time, and UCLA taught

Farsi language classes. Our community in New Zealand is tiny in comparison. In 2013, the New Zealand census recorded just over 3000 people identifying as Iranian.

Growing up in New Zealand, I was always highly aware of being 'different'. Back in Iran I was a chatterbox, never shutting up and continually forcing adults to listen to my dull stories. In New Zealand, the language I was so comfortable with had to be set aside and a new one learned quickly. This silenced me so much that I became a more shy and reserved person. I began to see how others would view me as different, whether it was because of my name or how I looked. However, my childlike resilience and inability to dwell on these things for long gave me the courage to ignore them. I made good friends quickly and it was through them that I learned about New Zealand culture. Rose Lu in her book notes how she learned about American and British children through watching films and reading books. I learned about New Zealand through my friends.

I remember joining the field hockey team because Amanda was in the team; during the first game I was thrown in to chase the ball without any idea of how the game was played. My parents, standing at the sidelines in the cold drizzle, were also bemused at what this sport was. At primary school I became a master daredevil, attempting death-defying choreography on the jungle bars and flying higher than anyone else on the maypoles. In high school I would skip school to go be bored at the mall and spend weekends at slumber parties rocking out to terrible pop music. I got my driver's licence at fifteen and became a prefect in my final year of high school. I had my own milestone birthday parties including a very drunken twenty-first and a more casual thirtieth. I went flatting with friends in my twenties and worked every terrible underpaid job made for youth workers. It is the privilege of 1.5- and second-generation migrants to be able to fully immerse themselves in this way.

I do wonder what my life would have been like had I grown up in Iran. No doubt certain aspects of my life would have been very different, but I do not think the values I hold, nor my personality, would have changed.

—

In the mid-nineties, New Zealand First MP Winston Peters infamously warned of an 'Asian invasion' and later in 2017 wrote this absolute banger: 'Immigration is great for immigrants. They've hit paradise compared to where they've come from.' Over in Australia, another politician cried to the television cameras that Australia was in danger of being 'swamped by Asians' and in later years wore a full burqa to Parliament to symbolise her opposition to allowing Muslim women to wear what they wanted. It seems that every decade a new group of immigrants is targeted for whatever ills society has, despite the fact that many of these immigrants have had ancestors in New Zealand for decades. In 2020, I directed a short documentary series on Muslim New Zealanders entitled *This is Us*. One of the women we interviewed, Latifa Daud, recalled the story of her great-great-grandfather leaving Gujarat, India for Auckland on a boat in 1908. He worked in the Waikato and had to endure years of blatant systemic racism such as landlords refusing to rent to him and signs outside establishments citing 'No Indians or Chinese'. She would tell me the anger she felt whenever someone would state that Aotearoa was not her home because of her ethnicity. Her family had lived in Aotearoa for over a century and yet they were still being told to 'go home'.

The first record of Iranians in New Zealand, according to New Zealand Internal Affairs, notes how there were seventeen citizenships awarded to Iranians (who had Iranian citizenship) between 1949 and 1979, prior to the 1979 revolution. Only in 1993 did that number reach triple digits, with the highest number of citizenships, 239, awarded in 2007 (Citizenship Statistics). Overall, 4380 citizenships were awarded to Iranians between 1949 and

2017. Of course, many people do not take up citizenship, so the numbers for those identifying as Iranian would most likely be higher. Though the spike in arrivals seems recent, the 'Birthplace and sex by years since arrival in New Zealand' denotes that the majority of Iranians came between 1987 (near the end of the Iran–Iraq war) and 1996.

In my Catholic primary school we were asked to trace our ancestral lineage and present it to the class. On the first day, nearly all of the Pākehā kids presented their detailed reports, each noting the various European countries their great-grandparents and great-great-grandparents came from.

'That makes me one-quarter Irish, one-quarter English and half-Scottish!' the girl with the long golden hair declared. She had become my nemesis after outright refusing to take my card inviting her to my birthday party, citing that it was the same day as her birthday. I realised she was lying when I saw the class chart outlining everyone's birthdays on the wall. Deep in my heart, though, I still yearned for her to be my friend and so when I ran home that day, I practically yelled at my mother to tell me how much more Scottish or Irish we were than she was.

'We're just Persian,' my mum replied, meticulously vacuuming the same bit of carpet over and over again.

'No, I mean, way back, like where are our great-great-grandparents from?' I asked in desperation.

'Persia. They're all from Iran,' she replied, still not very interested.

'No! I mean ages ago!'

'Persia! We're from Persia! It's one of the oldest civilisations in the world, now let me clean!' she yelled, clearly annoyed at my ignorance.

'You don't understand!' I yelled back and stormed off to my room to sulk.

Thirty years later I sent my DNA to an online ancestry site, excited to see the various surprising results I would get like my friends—maybe 30 per cent Indian or 5 per cent North African? Excited and optimistic, I opened my page to see '100 per cent Persia/Iran'.

No one I knew had ever got exactly 100 per cent. When I told my mum, she merely replied with, 'I told you.'

Brown
Girl
in the
Ring

A man wearing ram antlers stares at his victim. His eyes widen as the red under-light throws monstrously sharp shadows across his face. A choir of voices sings eerily in the background. The man's voice deepens as the choir gets louder, their chanting becoming more and more ominous like the tragic climax from an opera. The man's hand hovers across the victim's trembling chest. Suddenly the man twists his hand, shoves it deep into the victim's chest and rips out his still-beating heart. The victim screams as the choir cries in unison. The man holds up the heart as it continues to beat in his hand. The victim has no time to comprehend this black magic. He is lowered into a pit of molten lava where he then burns to death. His beating heart bursts into flames as Mola Ram laughs and his horde of followers celebrates. Indiana Jones looks on, astonished and alarmed.

The Indiana Jones films follow a heroic archaeologist who goes on adventures to often 'exotic' lands where he encounters many forms of evil, including ferocious snakes in pits, ferocious Nazis and ferocious cults in India. Much of the franchise takes inspiration from swashbuckling studio films of the 1930s where Western men would venture overseas into deserts and rainforests in order to bring a type of Western 'civility' to the 'savages' that lived there. Both George Lucas and Steven Spielberg, who created Indy, note these white saviour films as influences but both also note that *Indiana Jones and the Temple of Doom* (1984) was their darkest and most problematic film. For the filmmakers, the problems were mainly story issues where the narrative seems to jump all over the place. For me, the real problem is the barbarity with which India and Indians were so harshly depicted. As in the case of the early swashbuckling films, these films were written and created by people who barely knew anything about the cultures they were supposedly describing and so relied on stereotypes and clichés to give them dramatic beats. *Temple of Doom* is one of the most grotesque films I've ever seen, and its traumatic effect on me, as a child, has stayed deep within.

Temple of Doom mainly takes place in (a demented and fictional) 1930s India wherein Indy and his mates must help some poor villagers bring back their children who have been kidnapped and enslaved to work in mines for a sacrificial cult, which worships the goddess Kali. Alongside the terrifying heart scene is the infamous state dinner where a prepubescent maharaja brings Indy and his gang supposed local delicacies of snakes and monkey brains, complete with monkey heads, for them to eat. This film deeply affected my thinking. It made me believe that Indian people eat monkey brains for dinner and tore out their own people's beating hearts as a way to appease their gods.

These fabrications fed into my already growing distaste for anyone brown due to the dislike I had for anyone who did not fit into the ideal look—that is, anyone who was not white-skinned and blond-haired and looked like MacGyver. This dislike brewed a contempt in me for India and Indians in particular because people would often think I was from India. Of course, I didn't know anything about the beauty of such a place, its history, its cultures, its languages, its food, or its inventions, creations and leaders. I didn't understand my own internalised racism. I just didn't want to be brown and different; I wanted to be like everyone else. I wanted to be white.

This incessant need to be like everyone else is not just a cultural thing attributed to immigrant kids. It seems universal for nearly all children because anything that sets them apart from the herd can be used as a cause to mock. Kids are not always mean, but when they are, they can be vicious.

When we first arrived in New Zealand, my parents only knew Aunt Rose and Amir, but in a surprising twist of fate another young Iranian couple with a baby son moved in next door. Through each other the two couples began meeting other recently arrived Iranian immigrants, all young urban professionals who had managed to escape Iran in the 1980s as migrants or refugees. The group began to find solace in each other. It was unlikely that they would ever have crossed paths back home in Iran: some of my parents' new friends came from completely different geographical regions and worked in unrelated professional fields—there were pilots, architects and primary school teachers—and many belonged to varying political factions in the revolution (from leftist Marxists to conservative monarchists). Despite these differences in their pasts they forged deep friendships, many of which continue to this day.

My parents and their friends would socialise at every chance they could as they formed their own little community. They would take turns having parties at home, or what we call a *mehmooni*/مهمانی. They would drink whisky and put on cassettes from the homeland, as it was near impossible to find any new Persian music in a place like Aotearoa. While the real Iran continued moving forward (or backwards in other ways), my parents' cultural references and memories stayed frozen to the time before they left. They continually played music from the mid-1980s and referenced famous stars from their youth like legendary Iranian pop star Googoosh and French actor Alain Delon.

This was a time when many people in New Zealand had never even heard of Iran, constantly mistaking it for a misspelt Iraq, and kids would often ask me if Saddam Hussein was my dad. In the US, during this time, the ongoing poor relations between the US and Iran was the cause of much anti-Iranian rhetoric due to the hostage situation. We were spared the direct racism our cousins in the US were subjected to—from the banal, such as bumper stickers 'Nuke Iran', 'Fuck Iran' and 'Don't waste Gas/ Waste Khomeini', to hordes of protesters yelling 'Camel jockeys go home!' and even a highly successful pop song, 'Bomb Iran' by Vince Vance & The Valiants, sung to the tune of 'Barbara Ann' popularised by The Beach Boys. That same gruesome song was inexplicably resurrected during John McCain's failed presidential run in 2008.

My parents' friends also had young children whom Baby Sister and I made close friends with. These kids also understood some of our challenges that our Kiwi friends didn't—like having strict parents, not wearing shoes in the house and how you always needed to take a nap after indulging in Persian kebabs, whatever the time of day. One of my first-ever best friends was Shirin, whom I would see nearly every week when our parents got together. The first time we met, both of our families were at Long Bay beach and Shirin jumped on the flying fox, fell straight off and cut her lip. I thought she was super brave.

Soon our little twosome became a foursome when two other girls, both born in the same year as us, joined. We even had a couple of boys around our age join too, and so when our parents were busy in the living room, drinking, smoking and dancing to some relic 1980s Persian pop song, we would all huddle in a bedroom and play games. Truth or Dare was an obvious favourite, though when that inevitable question came up of who you fancied, it got fairly dire as we could only choose from these two poor boys. One of the other girls, Golriz, was relatively new when her parents moved to New Zealand in 1990. We were at another *mehmooni* and ten-year-old Golriz was sitting alone in her oversized floral dress, terrified of all of the strangers around her. My aunt asked me to befriend her. I reluctantly did so, as I already had one Iranian friend and another might upset the balance. I immediately told her how I was going to become a successful actress one day.

She replied, 'Cool.'

We then bonded after harassing one of the boys and have been good friends ever since.

Sleepovers seem like a rite of passage for pre-teen girls and I absolutely loved them. It was like flatting with your best friends but without the reality of having to pay rent and bills. The agenda would usually include meticulously going through every page in a teen magazine, the sealed sex sections being the most popular. Even though we had no experience in this area, we would still howl with laughter at the inexplicable sex tips *Cosmo* or *Dolly* magazine fixated on, which for a women's magazine seemed far too obsessed with blowjobs than anything else.

On one of these sleepover nights we decided to call up one of our male Iranian friends and, riled up on sugar and nonsensical sex tips, we started talking to his mates who were over at his place. At some point, we all wrote down detailed notes of what each of us looked like so we could explain all in careful detail to the boys. Here are the actual descriptions I later found in my diary:

> *Vanise: brown chocolate hair, green eyes*
> *Erica: Light brown hair, green eyes*
> *Summer: Platinum blonde hair, blue eyes*
> *Kelly: Strawberry blonde hair, blue eyes.*

We asked the boys what they looked like and sure enough we too were hit with descriptions of Aryan princes and mini models who all seemed to be blond, white and blue-eyed.

We were giddy with excitement and this insanity continued for some time. Back then, calling someone at home could mean hours on the phone. Understandably, the boys soon got tired of this incessant chatting from girls they didn't know and clearly didn't want to know. We finally called our friend back to get some answers. Annoyed, he quickly replied that it was just him and two mates making things up. There was no hotter older brother who surfed on weekends and the two mates were actually called Rajesh and Suraj. They were brown like us. Years later, when Golriz and I would recall this particular story, we would share a laugh but also mild revulsion at just how much ideologies around Western beauty and whiteness were entrenched within us, even as children.

The next year I started at intermediate school. The obscure in-between school you attend for only two years. The school was nestled among some state housing and a small shopping centre with the oddest mix of stores—a multibillion-dollar bank, a takeaway named after a mythological dragon and the 'health shop'. The health shop was our favourite store as they sold health supplements and protein shakes, but also one-cent and five-cent lollies.

Unlike the high school I would attend in two years, the intermediate had a great mix of the community including many Māori and Pasifika kids. Infuriatingly, it was known as a 'ghetto' school because many of the students came from the neighbouring state-housing area and/or sported darker melanin than the other schools in the district. Even at that age it was hard to escape systemic racism.

One particular event was folk dancing practice. In primary school, I despised this medieval monstrosity because every time Boney M's song 'Brown Girl in the Ring' was played, some genius would think it hilarious to shove me into the centre of a circle like it was a Victorian freak show as the rest of the children would clap and sing along. Ever since then I have no patience for any form of disco music.

English folk dancing was apparently introduced into New Zealand primary schools in the 1930s as a form of exercise. It often required us all to find a partner of the opposite sex (only gender binaries in the nineties!) and dance, though nothing went beyond some risqué hand-holding. In one year at intermediate, I remember a few of the Pākehā girls in my group were partnered up with some of the 'brown' boys. The girls were terrible actors and the disgust that spread across their faces was obvious. Without even blinking, each girl stretched the sleeves on her red woollen school jersey down as far as she could, to cover her hands like gloves before touching the boys. Wanting to fit in, and without even thinking of the deeper reasons or the mere sadistic irony, I pulled my jersey down to cover my precious hands before holding hands with my partner. The poor boy who was forced to endure this humiliation noticed straight away. He was one of the naughty kids at school who was forever getting into trouble, mainly because he was double the size of every other kid there. His statuesque figure contrasted with his baby cheeks and soft face. And it was this face that was suddenly crestfallen when he saw what I did. Despite his years of being the rebel and the fighter, the 'bad boy' and the academic anarchist, this moment utterly crushed him. I remember thinking something was not right but with my limited self-awareness I could not pinpoint it. To that boy today, and all of those boys in our circle, I am sorry. To the girls in my circle who initiated it, I hope you never forget it and that you regret it to the end of your days, as I will.

Unsurprisingly, I too began to have experiences where my darker melanin was a cause of concern for some and ridicule for others. During athletics day at primary school, I joined the sprinting team. At that time I was tiny with skinny legs and arms which contrasted with my mass of black hair. My small face barely peeped out from beyond the two thick eyebrows that protruded proudly. I loved the sprint race and remember running as fast as my tiny frame would allow, smiling at how well I was doing until some joker decided to call me Speedy Gonzales. Soon, the entire class followed and a chorus of pre-teen voices bellowed, 'Go Speedy! Go Speedy!'

I never entered athletics again.

A year later I decided to take up rhythmic gymnastics, as I loved the combination of dance and flexibility. I practised every day and finally began winning national competitions. Yet I was always aware of how different I looked to the other girls. Gymnastics in the early 1990s was not a diverse sport. When I look back at the photos my parents took, no doubt bored at having to spend their Saturdays watching other people's children spin ribbons, I stand out like a tiny brown thumb. At the time I thoroughly believed the other girls were judging me not for my athletic abilities but for the colour of my skin and thick hair.

Speedy Gonzales could never become a gymnast. He could never even become a fully-fledged character. Speedy Gonzales was a caricature; always wearing his yellow sombrero, speaking with an exaggerated 'Mexican accent' and hanging out with lazy drunken mice during the day.

On the DVD box sets, there is now a disclaimer, to make up for past 'offences' by the company: 'The cartoons you are about to see are products of their time.' Perhaps, but Speedy first came to our screens in the 1950s, and I was getting ridiculed forty years later. They were racist then, just as they are racist now.

—

Like many kids growing up, I was hyper aware of the way I looked. Even if someone praised my looks, I would still hate my skin and hair. The numerous and endless beauty regimes I endured to straighten my hair, or bleach my facial hair and even my eyebrows, are all sadly commonplace with many women of colour. I had actual friends innocently mock me for my facial hair, not realising how deeply shameful it felt to have to torment my body into fitting beauty ideals that these friends just naturally met. Even recently, I was wading through the foundations at the Estée Lauder counter at Auckland Airport and the salesperson kindly, but bluntly, told me how they did not store any dark shades as the majority of their customers were 'Asian'. Another time, in Canada, I was meeting with an acting agent who seemed interested in representing me but had to note that I was 'too dark to pass for Iranian'. Instead I should learn how to 'do

Indian accents' for potential roles. I laughed in his face and never signed up.

During my years at intermediate, I fell in love with the teen franchise *Sweet Valley High*. This was a highly popular book series created by Francine Pascal that centred on two identical teenage sisters who had completely different personalities. The whole series revolved around American high-school stereotypes and sometimes very questionable plot points. Every book of the 100 written begins with a detailed description of the twins, who both had 'shoulder-length blonde hair, blue-green eyes, and perfect California tans'. They would date blond quarterbacks called Ken or guys with 'piercing blue eyes' like rich boy Bruce Patman. This series played directly into my own obsessions: not only did I want to be white, I also wanted a white man. It's no secret to my friends (and a source of much ridicule) that my default for finding someone attractive in the dating world is the real-life Ken doll.

Recently I had a conversation with a fellow filmmaker, herself from an Asian background; I told her this theory of mine, that my ideals had been shaped because of the books I read and the films I watched of white, blond-haired Prince Charmings. She replied that for her it was about power. She believes that our attraction to this type of idealised man is because of the power these men hold in society. Because no matter how successful we will become, our place in society will never be on a par with these white men.

As children, Golriz and I adored playing with Barbies. Like puppet masters with our own willing actors, we would dress them up and make them act out scenarios. Golriz's favourite was a blonde-haired, blue-eyed Wedding Barbie. She used to rip the wedding dress off straight away as vindication that we didn't care much about marriage. My favourite was Hawaiian Barbie. She wore sparkly blue shorts and a matching crop top, but most importantly, she was brown with brown curly hair. In hindsight it was a rather problematic attempt on the manufacturer's part to sell her as 'tanned Barbie', but for me this slight variation in her plastic colour made all the difference. I never got a Ken doll, much to my dismay.

—

People often fail to understand the importance of words like ethnicity and race. They complain about buzzwords like 'identity politics' or 'people of colour' because they fear that which they do not understand. The concept of race as we know it was unheard of in ancient Egypt, Greece or Rome. Harlon Dalton, in his essay on white privilege, says that ethnicity is what we pride ourselves on when considering aspects of our culture: language, customs, rituals and even cuisines. More importantly, ethnicity can exist on its own. In contrast, race needs comparisons in order to have meaning. He notes how it becomes easy not to think about race when you are the dominant race. That is an example of white privilege.

I often think about this when facing racism today. A few years ago I was reading the national current affairs magazine *North & South*. One of the main articles featured a survey taken of New Zealanders and what they believed were 'true Kiwi values'. The respondents rated tolerance and equality as two of the highest values. The survey then focused on questions about immigration. Not surprisingly, there were widely contrasting and hypocritical findings, not to mention very dubious questions to begin with. When asked if Aotearoa was letting in too many immigrants, the majority of respondents answered yes. The survey then gave respondents ethnic categories for which immigrants they would prefer to allow in and, not surprisingly, the majority voted a resounding yes to those originating from Europe and a giant no to those from Asia. Tolerant and equal indeed.

This survey infuriated me so much so that I wrote a long email to the editor citing the hypocrisies of the piece and detailing my own experiences. The editor was elated to have such a response; she granted it letter of the month and even mentioned my letter in her editorial (though she weirdly labelled me as a 'dark-skinned and funny-named foreigner'). What I wanted to point out in the letter was that no matter how hard someone might try to be 'a Kiwi' (whatever that is), they would never be seen as one due to the colour of their skin and their 'funny-sounding' name. Assimilation does not work. In fact, assimilation is cultural genocide. You cannot ask someone to fully assimilate into a culture and completely eradicate their own.

'You're a Kiwi now.'

'Go home if you don't like it here.'

'But you have to like rugby!'

Recently on a chat show actor Whoopi Goldberg reminisced about her early years in show business, specifically about the one-woman theatre show she had created that brought her to the attention of filmmaker Steven Spielberg. Her show included a segment about E.T., the alien character from one of Spielberg's most famous films, *E.T. the Extra-Terrestrial* (1982). In Goldberg's show, E.T. doesn't return home to his planet but instead he stays on Earth and becomes a gangster. He grows Jheri curls and wears gold jewellery, and when his family finally arrives in the spaceship, he shoots them all in a fury of gunfire. He kills them because he doesn't recognise them. He doesn't recognise them because he has assimilated into being human, so much so that he has forgotten his own roots.

Assimilation means erasing your identity and past, and everything that has made you who you are. Integration is different. Integration asks you to include yourself in society as yourself. It does not ask you to murder your past.

The Girl
from
Revolution
Road

On a chilly December day in 2017, a young Iranian woman, Vida, makes her way through the bustling busy streets of Tehran, the capital city of Iran. She holds her white hijab on her head with one hand and a long stick in the other. She avoids eye contact with the hundreds of bodies that move past her. She remains focused and determined and so continues to gaze at the concrete pavement below to avoid any distractions. At a busy intersection she is finally forced to look up to make her way across. Cars stop and honk, motorbikes zoom dangerously close as she strides out, stopping every now and then as motorists and pedestrians zigzag in a tight dance. Vida almost makes it across as a white van suddenly screeches before her. She glances at the driver who merely nods and holds his hand up politely. Vida smiles and quickly scampers past to the safety of the pavement on the other side.

Vida spots the perfect position on the edge of the pavement. A small utility box peeps from beneath the hordes of people walking past. She jumps on it quickly, her white sneakers supporting her agility. Vida stands tall in her matching black tracksuit. A few heads glance up at her, but most stay glued to their destinations or their phones, ignoring her. Vida closes her eyes, takes a deep breath and slowly but meticulously removes her white hijab completely. Her dark hair ripples down her back as if sighing with pent-up relief. She stares into the distance, refusing to make eye contact in case someone begs her to change her mind. Vida wraps the white hijab around her stick and holds it up as a soldier does with their rifle. Vida continues to stare past the hijab down the main avenue Enghelab Street/خیابان انقلاب or Revolution Road, which had once been called Shah Reza Avenue after the former monarch. In her periphery she can see some people looking up at her, mouths gaping. A young man nearby takes a photo on his phone. Others keep walking past. A couple of older men jeer, while a couple of women clap. No one dares to stop for too long for fear of being associated with her. Vida stays completely motionless, holding her stance as a silent warrior.

After her image went viral all around the world, she became known as 'The Girl from Revolution Road'.

—

When I returned to London in 2009, I was determined to make the city my permanent home. I had worked hard to save money so I could be granted a three-year highly skilled migrant visa. The dream was to gain a prestigious London agent, find a hot boyfriend that looked like Brit rugby star Jonny Wilkinson and live in some cute but extortionately overpriced studio flat in cool Brixton. However, as they say in *The Adventures of Priscilla, Queen of the Desert*, 'Assumption, my dear Mitz, is the mother of all fuck-ups.' In reality, I ended up having a terrible falling-out with a friend and flatmate; I failed to find work due to the 2008 recession; I had my heart broken; and at one point I had to sleep on a blanket in my friends' lounge. I lasted nine months and returned home, broken but not defeated.

While in London, my friend Yoong decided to join me and together we gallantly became model tourists by visiting sites like Hampton Court Palace, the Houses of Parliament and the Museum of London to fully engage with our inner historian nerds. We also visited Yoong's 'Aunt' Kimmy who lived in Colchester with her English husband John. Like Yoong, Kimmy also grew up in Malaysia but her parents came from Hainan Island, the southernmost point in mainland China. They lived near

Yoong's grandad who was known for two things: fishing and being terrified of the Japanese. He'd been shot in the arse by a Japanese soldier and taken to an internment camp during World War II. His love of fishing came from eating only boiled bark soup after being trapped in the jungle by soldiers. He would often make Yoong's father and his brothers take freshly caught fish to Kimmy's family.

Yoong and I absolutely adored Kimmy and John. Their home was full of books and stylish furniture, a far cry from the sad flat-pack beige furniture that seems to pop up in every rental in London. Kimmy and John were both big foodies and so we enjoyed an endless array of delicious cuisine and fresh food, which if you have ever been on a limited income is a luxury. They were both big talkers and full of love and life. They had at least thirty-something years on us, but their energy was intoxicating. Kimmy even told us of the day she received her OBE (Officer of the Most Excellent Order of the British Empire) from the Queen.

'What was she like?' we asked.

'Fine. She had fat ankles,' Kimmy replied.

Kimmy was a professor who helped establish the Nursing and Health Studies Unit at the University of Essex and was a leader in healthcare, advocating and strengthening the relationship of the National Health

Service with healthcare graduates. Seeing how Kimmy and John lived, how they had accomplished so much over the decades, and how they were still loving it all, made me rethink my career trajectory. Suddenly, I could see myself living like a professor and I loved it.

Sadly, Kimmy died from a brain aneurysm a few years later. John visited us in New Zealand; he spent his time travelling and visiting his grandkids in London. They say you never know when inspiration will hit, and I believe now that you also never know who could provide that inspiration. Even though we only met a handful of times, it was because of Kimmy that I decided to return to Aotearoa and resume my studies.

The first year I attended university was 1999, on the cusp of the new millennium. I disliked it, believing university to be a place of greys and eternal darkness from which no light shone. Hyperbole or not, that is typical of seeing the world from the midst of a major depressive episode. Eleven years later I was back there again to undertake my master of arts. I was a bit older, a bit wiser and more motivated to tackle tertiary study, and like the usual 'mature' student I would sit in the front of lectures and ask questions, finally loving learning. In 2010, I decided to focus my master's thesis on a documentary on Iran. Living in the UK, the US and also a brief stint in

Canada had made me question the idea of home. When people would ask me that inevitable question of where I was from, I would reply New Zealand, at which I would often be met with confusion. If I answered Iran, they would congratulate me on my excellent English. One time in Italy, I had an intense argument with an elderly woman about how I lived in London, but was from New Zealand, *and* from Iran. She vigorously insisted I was Spanish.

My thesis short film was *Iran in Transit* (2012), an auto-ethnographic documentary that followed my journey back to Iran from New Zealand; my first visit in decades. The premise explored the idea of home and homelands through my own perspectives and findings. The main question was what constitutes a home and if a homeland is even relevant to immigrants like me. I was born in Iran but grew up in New Zealand, so would Iran still be considered my home? What is a homeland? Based on popular rhetoric, for me it would be Iran, as it is my ancestral home and many of its cultural values are still with me, such as the language, customs and even some of the traditions. And yet, I found it difficult to engage with a sense of homeland as it clashed with my idea of a home. Most of my memories are in New Zealand where I have spent the majority of my life. Therefore, the question became: is my homeland the place where I was born, but know little about? Or is my home the place to which my family immigrated and where I hold the most memories?

The first time I returned to Iran, I was thirteen years old and in my first year of high school. It took three planes and almost two days to reach Iran from New Zealand. My whole family went and although I enjoyed meeting my cousins, whom I had not seen for over a decade, I hated the trip. I hated that we had to continually visit people I had never heard of. I hated that I couldn't understand the language as well as my cousins. I hated that we didn't do anything touristy. Most of all I hated wearing a hijab.

The hijab is one example of the veil which has become such a prominent motif of the Middle East; it requires some historical context.

The veil has been a part of women's dress in both Western and Eastern cultures for centuries, from Egyptian goddesses to the Christian veiled Mary in Renaissance paintings. In Ancient Persia, the veil was in use throughout the Sassanid and Byzantine empires as a fashion statement until it became attire for religious women after the Arab conquests in the seventh century. Under Reza Shah, Western dress (or non-Islamic attire) became one of his most controversial acts when he outlawed the chador (a long fabric that covers everything but the face) in 1936. Women, including those who were non-religious, took to veiling as a form of political protest against his son, Reza Shah Pahlavi, in the 1960s and 1970s; when Ayatollah Khomeini came to power, he initiated the idea of mandatory veiling as a 'recommendation' in 1980 until it became law in 1983. By 1986 the punishment for not veiling included public lashings and imprisonment, punishments which are still used today.

What is important to note is that, contrary to belief, neither forced unveiling or veiling improved the status of women in society. Instead, it merely highlighted the vast differences among them. For example, the majority of those who were unveiled were often educated, middle-class and elite urbanites, while many who took to the veil were either illiterate or educated at home, religious and living in rural areas. After the 1979 regime change, women who did not adhere to the veil were seen as puppets or dolls of the 'evil West' and their punishments were enforced by the newly founded police unit, the Komiteh. A 'bad hijab' could constitute anything from partial veiling to tight clothing and makeup, which was thought to encourage the male gaze.

The Komiteh's work was strongly in evidence during the Iran–Iraq war of 1980–88, as upholding the veil became a weapon to control the country during the chaos. As many men (and boys) were sent to the front line, women were expected to also play a role. The war made the hijab an important propaganda tool: the veiled woman became the symbol of bringing up new generations of 'pious' children who would eventually become martyrs for the nation, as many did during the revolution. Martyrdom and the role of the good wife and holy mother play an integral role in Islamic ideology as in Christianity.

Posters, murals and stamps showed women in chadors and hijabs, standing behind their sons, brothers and husbands as they prepared to go to battle. Some posters even showed women in black chadors proudly holding guns. The veiled woman as a *jihadi* and a martyr thus became synonymous, for outsiders, with images of Iran.

After the war, although the Komiteh lost some of its power, the law remained and ideology shifted to the veil as a symbol of a moral woman. During the Green Movement in 2009, whereby thousands took to the streets in protest against the re-election of President Mahmoud Ahmadinejad, the veil was once again converted into a tool of resistance. Women were unveiling in public (still punishable by fines and imprisonment) as a form of protest, just as women had worn the veil in protest against the Shah before and during the revolution.

This history of the veil in Iran is important to remember when thinking of how many Iranians in the diaspora respond to it and to Islam in general. Many who left were not religious, and so being forced to wear an item of clothing in order to signify one's morality imprinted a deep distaste for the hijab. I used to be one of those Iranians who believed that a woman would never truly choose to wear such a thing, because the only relationship I had with the hijab was one of force. Later, I realised that it was not the hijab that was to blame, but the lack of choice. Forcing women to veil or unveil strips them of agency over their own bodies. There are still prominent Iranians in the diaspora today who jump on the Islamophobic bandwagon and denounce all veilings as oppressive and 'un-Western'. Much of this makes sense when we think of how traumatised and fearful women in Iran were made to feel about covering up, particularly in the early years of the regime change. However, there are plenty of women who choose to veil as a way to express their dedication to their faith.

In 2010, I set off to Iran on my own. I used my New Zealand passport to travel to Dubai, where I changed to my Iranian passport to gain entry into Iran. On the two-hour, alcohol-free Emirates flight, it was an odd sight to see the unveiled women passengers suddenly grabbing their scarves and gloomily putting them on before we landed at Imam Khomeini International Airport in

Tehran. Departing from the plane, I was immediately hit with unusual smells and the air itself felt foreign. It was dry and yet humid at the same time. A slight tang of something old hung about, possibly symbolising the oppressive atmosphere. The airport was not very busy and nothing felt modern. My cousin Ellie met me at the gate.

Ellie and her family moved to Canada when she was a teenager. She continued to wear a hijab as a promise to her grandfather before he died. For years Ellie was mocked and harassed for wearing a hijab but she fought back and in later years stopped wearing it. Even though she enjoyed her lifestyle in Canada, she missed Iran and later returned with her parents and two brothers. Ellie and I were born only two months apart and if we had been able to stay in the same country growing up, no doubt we would have been inseparable. When our youngest uncle got married in San Francisco, both our families attended and then took a vacation to Disneyland. For the longest time I didn't understand why Ellie and her family would only eat vegetarian burgers, and suddenly take to prayer in the middle of the Magic Kingdom, much to the confusion of other park dwellers. There was much about this faith that I did not know.

My earliest memory of religion in general remains with my grandmother on my father's side. A stout but extremely huggable woman—something she has in common with many grandmothers—Mamanoo, as we affectionately call her, is now pushing ninety and still going strong. She will leap at any opportunity to dance despite her weak knees and slow speed, and she still dyes her hair a chestnut brown whenever she can. I remember watching Mamanoo, draped in her white chador and sitting on her colourful mat covered in florals. She would whisper her prayers and turn her rosary before bending down and placing her head at the *turbah* (a piece of clay symbolising earth) three times. As a four-year-old, I would try to imitate her. Grabbing a bedsheet, I would wrap it around my tiny frame, the sheet often tangling itself. I had no idea what she was saying and so would mumble nonsense as a form of prayer then bend and pray.

Mamanoo lived in a small town called Shahmirzad/ شهمیرزاد located north of Tehran and below the Alborz mountains. It was one of those places where everyone knew everyone, and so when a cousin introduced her to our grandfather (whom we affectionately called Babajoon) they already knew each other's families. Mamanoo and Babajoon wed sometime during World War II. At one point they lived in the US to be closer to their six children and many grandchildren, though they barely left their apartment. They knew no English and spent their days watching Mexican soap operas dubbed in Farsi on satellite television from Dubai. My family tells me when my grandfather was on his deathbed years ago back in Iran, he began speaking something resembling broken Russian, his Alzheimer's having taken over. My dad did not see him before he passed away. We hurriedly bought him an Emirates ticket so that he could take the three planes required to be at the funeral.

My mother's mum stayed in Iran her entire life until she passed away in the mid-2000s. My mother was not able to make her funeral. It is a sombre thought to realise just how distant living in exile and away from family can be. In Iran, I visited my grandmother's grave with my Aunt Nasrine. It was a simple grey, coffin-sized plaque sunk into the ground, in a line of identical grey plaques, near a highway. Beautiful calligraphy adorned her epitaph, but I could not read it. It was an uncanny feeling being at her gravesite, knowing who she was and who she represented but having missed all those years being her granddaughter. A young man sat at a nearby grave, his head in his hands, teary-eyed. He was mourning his father.

—

Ellie and her family are quite wealthy and so their lifestyle represents a very different type to that of the average

Iranian. Ellie's family-owned apartment block is in the more affluent North Tehran and with her I am able to see what life is like for the rich Tehrani youth who often have nothing more to do than to live in ennui and spend their millions in a country where more than half its people are aged under thirty-five.

The first thing Ellie tells me is that she always carries a US$50 note with her in case she needs to bribe an official. Iran, like so many other countries living in the chaos that follows a revolution, is corrupt. A friend told us how he was nearly kicked out of the Basij force, the paramilitary religious sect that many people fear. He joined to lessen the number of months needed to complete mandatory military training. He was nearly arrested at a party by the Basij as he was chatting to a girl and it took him a while to convince them that he was indeed one of them, a fellow 'brother'. Ellie's friends tell me that anything is possible in Iran if you have enough money to bribe officials. You could even organise a naked tennis tournament on the roof of your apartment block while paying off police below to keep away the Basij. Alcohol is of course banned, but so are mixed gatherings of women and men.

These regulations are indicative of the arbitrary rules autocratic regimes impose on people in order to uphold their power. Yet it seems that this power can only last for so long before people begin challenging and outright fighting it.

At first wearing the hijab takes practice. Ellie is a master at teaching me how to wear it in a more trendy way with it hanging very loosely around the head so most of the forehead and even part of the crown is exposed. One half of the scarf is then folded into the other shoulder. Never tie it or, God forbid, you'll look 'cheap'. The hijab felt like an invading force stuck on my head. I often forgot that I needed to wear it, which gave me flashbacks to my early days in Iran, when six years old. In our class, the teacher let us unveil but many a time I forgot to put it back on once recess started.

Soon, though, wearing the veil becomes just another uniform. Unlikeable, symbolically problematic, but for most days, tolerable. In Tehran many women have found ways to rebel against this mandatory uniform. They wear heavy makeup, show off their 'new' surgically enhanced noses and reveal as much of their hair as possible, unless a Basij cop is around, then they must quickly pull the scarf down and avoid eye contact. Alongside the hijab, women and men must also cover their arms and legs. Often women will find fashionable coats and leggings daring to show some ankle. Despite having some of the harshest and strictest media censorship in the world, including banning most websites and social media, Iranians are allowed (legal) access to Instagram. There are hundreds if not thousands of accounts dedicated to showing off fashionistas around Iran, each delicately displaying their designer labels underneath their coats and their expensive highlights under their hijabs. After a few weeks of wearing something so rigid, I began to realise why women are so keen to individualise their appearance. It started to make sense that women experiment with makeup and hair and even facial piercings. To the horror of my mum, I got a nose piercing as a way to differentiate myself. This incessant need to express myself was so strong that it made me realise how easily I had taken it for granted in Aotearoa. Even when we decide to wear our sweatpants, Birks and two-week-old T-shirt, we are making a statement (albeit a lazy one). However, Iran is also a massive country of over eighty million inhabitants so in contrast to the colourful glitz of the fashion crowd, there are also women clad in simple black chadors showing only their paint-free faces and also women who refuse to partake in either look, and do their own thing.

Iran, like every other nation, is a patriarchy, but due to the 1979 constitution based on archaic Sharia law, women are classified as second-class citizens. They are half the worth of a man, or just his rib if we are being biblical.

They are discriminated against in the legal and judicial sphere, where a woman's testimony is worth half that of a man's and yet women are given harsher punishments than men when it comes to crimes of adultery and even murder. They cannot be president or in the clergy. And yet women in Iran, like those living under other autocratic regimes around the world, are fighting back. The literacy gap between men and women has lessened since 1979; women attend university and have careers, aside from domestic work, in most areas including law, medicine, business, communications and the humanities to name a few. In fact Iran supposedly has more women directors in the film industry than the US. There are Iranian women, known internationally, who are challenging the system, such as the human rights lawyer and Nobel Peace Prize winner Shirin Ebadi, and the young women activists working at the grassroots level such as Vida Movahedi, who protested without her hijab in 2017 and again in 2018, and as a result was arrested.

The first week in Iran, I was terrified of everything. Every day felt like the first day at high school when you're not sure about the rules and worry constantly that you're going to be told off. However, that feeling subsided very quickly. As there are no bars or clubs, house parties are common. Alcohol is easily bought on the black market and delivered to your apartment. I was drunk nearly every night of the second week, stumbling out of cars in my short dress that was barely covered by my long jacket, and holding my hijab on my head before letting it flutter off once inside. We drank, smoked and danced. In the numerous memoirs written by women in the Iranian diaspora, these underground parties are commonplace. This is the Iran most Westerners do not realise exists. This is the Iran that shows how the human spirit will fight oppression even through simple and menial ways in order to let people live.

—

My mum grew up with four sisters and one estranged brother who I didn't realise existed until only a few years ago. All of the sisters except one live in Aotearoa. Nasrine stayed in Iran but at one point made the move to Canada with her youngest daughter, Naz. The bitter cold climate and the challenges of learning a new language at the age of 60 proved too much and my aunt and cousin returned to Iran. The West is not always the magical Oz we perceive it to be. In fact, even the great and powerful Wizard was a fallacy and just some old ordinary bloke behind a giant curtain.

Nasrine and Naz now live in Karaj, a suburb an hour

out of Tehran. My aunt would spend her days as a retiree listening to the state radio and cursing it out loud while caring for their tiny Pomeranian affectionately nicknamed Freak. During my visit, I would spend the nights with Naz and her friend Hani, drinking whisky, smoking and listening to nineties rock. Some nights Naz and I would venture out in her car. Unlike me, Naz loves to drive. During a stint in Southern California where she studied for a year, she drove for Uber to make some cash. I thought it very brave, for Naz is tiny, with delicate porcelain-like features. In fact, Naz's personality is the opposite to her stature; staunch and resilient, she has a powerful sense of herself that could only have grown in a country like Iran. One night as we were driving, a police car drove up next to her, following her for a good distance. The cop would swap looks with her, his rugged face covered with a thick unkempt beard. Naz was stoic as she returned his look without flinching as I cowered in the passenger seat. He eventually drove off. Later Naz told me, 'You have to stare them down or they'll know you're scared.'

The week before I had arrived, Naz had been arrested by the Basij for having the Pomeranian in her car. The Basij said that the dog was drawing attention to her and that a 'pious' woman should never do such an immoral thing as to invite an unnecessary gaze. She was taken to a police cell where her father had to intervene, pay a bribe and bring her home. It is sadly common for women to be assaulted and even raped while in police custody. The police use this practice to incite fear and so are granted bribes by panicked parents who are rightly determined to save their daughters from such horrors.

—

New Zealand prime minister Jacinda Ardern wore a headscarf when visiting various mosques in Christchurch after the mosque attacks on 15 March 2019. This act drew conflicting opinions on whether or not her decision to wear the veil was the right one. Ardern's image in a hijab, eyes tightly closed and embracing a woman at the Kilbirnie Mosque in Wellington, went viral, so much so that the prime minister and ruler of the Emirate of Dubai plastered the image across the tallest building in the world, the Burj Khalifa in Dubai, as a thank you for her 'sincere empathy and support' for the world's Muslim population. A week later, women around the country took to wearing a headscarf as a form of solidarity with women who normally wear the veil and who have often faced discrimination because of it. Alongside strategic political reasons, the message was also to show Muslim women and Muslims in general that they were not alone.

This national day of solidarity drew even more contrasting views. An Iranian activist now living in exile, who runs a website that posts images of women in Iran protesting without hijabs, called it 'heartbreaking', while simultaneously numerous charities and organisations in New Zealand gave out free headscarves. Some called the gesture tokenistic. One prominent right-wing commentator condemned it as 'anti-feminist'. I chose not to wear a headscarf for I felt conflicted and thought that it would have been hypocritical for me to wear one. I wanted to show my respect for Muslim New Zealanders and their love of the faith, but I also wanted to show my support for the women activists in Iran who were risking their lives to protest its oppression. In that moment, the veil as a paradox was obvious.

On that day, the University of Auckland held a national day of remembrance. Many of us stood at the entrance of the university gym which had been made into a makeshift mosque, as Muslim students entered for Friday prayers. I watched a young woman in a colourful hijab help her friend put on a headscarf. Clearly the friend was a novice but the joy emanating from the woman wearing the hijab was so bright and dazzling that it all made sense. There is no doubt there would have been Muslim women who did not agree with this act of solidarity, but after witnessing the excitement on this young woman's face, I knew that there were many women who did appreciate it.

One of the most prominent Iranian artists living and working in the diaspora is photographer and filmmaker Shirin Neshat, who began her career after returning to Iran from studying in the US. On her return home, Neshat found herself being inspired by the martyred veiled woman that was so revered during the Iran–Iraq war. Neshat returned to the US, where she now lives in self-imposed exile, and her works often draw on the dual influences of her native Iran and her life in that in-between space of exile. In her photograph entitled *Rebellious Silence* (1994) from the series *Women of Allah* (1993–97), Neshat photographs herself in black and white, wearing a full black chador. She holds a rifle that is centred perfectly on her body and face, which is covered in Persian calligraphy reciting words from Iranian women writers and poets. Neshat's look is direct and confrontational, consciously complicating the viewer's gaze. As Neshat herself has stated, the gaze is paradoxical, much like the veil itself.

The veiled woman has become a symbol of Iran. The Pahlavi monarchy believed her to be a symbol of tradition and an antithesis to modernisation. Under the Islamic Republic she is the ideal to which all women must adhere: chaste, pious and an ally to the regime. In Western media, she is both oppressed and threatening. Women's bodies and how they choose to express themselves seem doomed to be continually in a tug of war between the patriarchy and the women who challenge it.

War
of
Terror

The first time I went to New York City, I was nineteen years old and on my own. Watching Hollywood films and American sitcoms while growing up made me yearn for the US, and I was near obsessed with moving there and living the idealised life I saw on screen. I wanted to attend a high school with decorated metal lockers and go home to a two-storey colonial house with a 'yard' and a bedroom window that good-looking, floppy-haired boys could throw pebbles at during the night to get my attention. I wanted to go to proms, date quarterbacks and attend homecoming (whatever the hell that was). I thoroughly believed that everything grand and wonderful lay in America, because at the time New Zealand was too small, too boring and none of the boys looked like Luke Perry. But, to be fair, no boy could look like Perry as he, like most of the cast of *Beverly Hills, 90210*, was a man in his mid-twenties playing a sixteen-year-old. I was so enamoured with the America I saw on screen that I developed a slight American accent, rolling my 'R's and becoming an expert at drawing the Stars and Stripes.

So it was with this joie de 'Murica that I worked three part-time jobs to save enough money to go on a work exchange over one New Zealand summer. The visa allowed any full-time tertiary student to work in the US in non-skilled work over a three- to four-month period. The visa was an incentive to get cheap, youthful labour to work in ski fields and summer camps. I went to live in Florida with my cousin and her husband. It meant that my parents would not worry about me, and I would not worry about having to pay rent or bills, something that terrified me right up to my thirties.

Iranian families are often closely knit. We will stay home until the end of days. It astounds me to hear of friends who were booted out of home at the ripe old age of eighteen. In contrast, a friend was shocked to hear I was going to be staying at my cousin's rent free for so long. For family to charge another family member would be ludicrous in Iranian culture. You might as well fake your own death and go and live in the mountains with goats, as that is how ostracised you would become. Money is capital and capitalism at its core is an individualistic venture.

Iranians, not unlike many Asian groups, are tribal and have been for centuries.

There are many hierarchies and cultural customs that we still abide by, like putting family first, simply because it's a nice way to live. There is a reason we love calling everyone within our community a 'cousin', 'uncle', or 'auntie', despite having no actual physical or legal relation. It becomes even more important when living in a different country that even meeting someone from the Iranian tribe can give you a slight rush of excitement. It may have something to do with the comfort in familiarity. After all, there is a reason we fear people and cultures we do not know.

My cousin Jasmine had married young to an older Iranian-American and they had a small apartment in the suburbs of Orlando where most of his family lived. Jasmine's family lived in Canada after enduring too many hardships while attempting to gain citizenship in the US. Unlike us, her family had fled Iran as asylum seekers. My aunt took her three younger children and Jasmine, a teenager at the time, with her. At one point they, alongside other asylum seekers, were held in a hotel by the FBI. One of the officers took a shine to Jasmine and so was overtly nice to the family. It's not difficult to see why. Jasmine is a tall brunette with long thick waves that shimmer down her back. She has had this same hair length ever since I have known her. She has wide brown eyes and a brilliant laugh.

I hadn't seen her for over twenty years and when we did meet again we bonded over our love of silly movies like *Office Space* and *Austin Powers*. Jasmine was the big sister I never had and we had the best time exploring the oddity of entertainment that Orlando is famous for, namely audacious theme parks and franchise restaurants where everything is dipped in fried batter. She did, however, refuse to attend a Backstreet Boys gig with me. That I attended alone, made friends with some intense fans and got kicked out of the Hard Rock Cafe for attempting to sneak backstage.

Jasmine and her husband were not a good match and this was evident from the very first day I stayed with them. It was intensely awkward to be present during one of their infamous arguments. These uncomfortable situations partly motivated me to take a trip to New York City along with another fellow Kiwi who was in the US. (In later years, Jasmine would finally divorce her husband and find her happily-ever-after with someone else.)

Travelling alone has its many perks and making friends, often in the most random places, is one. I met Kerrin at the Los Angeles Airport as a bunch of us fresh-faced Kiwis were finding our way to the beach-lined streets of Santa Monica. It's difficult not to want to be Kerrin's friend. Her extroverted ease at talking to strangers and her excitement at finally leaving Aotearoa was a great contrast to my usual introverted shyness. (Kerrin's confidence allowed her to take on some incredible goals and, as of now, she is one of the few Māori women on the Waitematā Local Board and has become the deputy chair, as well as being a Labour Party candidate for the Waikato.) When I met her, Kerrin was working on Catalina Island just off the California coast. We decided to meet up in New York City as neither of us had ever been to this legendary place. However, it was March and a snowstorm was looming. Many flights were postponed including Kerrin's, and so I ventured alone to one of the biggest cities in the world.

It was a bit of a disappointment when I first arrived at JFK. Airports, particularly in the US, are chaotic. Officials yell for no reason and everyone seems miserable. It was not the grand welcoming I was hoping for. I caught a bus to a hostel near Times Square, allowing me to see some of the Big Apple's sights: lots of brown brick buildings, dark skyscrapers and looming bridges. New York very quickly has a way of making one feel inferior.

The next day I spent completely alone, wandering the streets, which were now covered in ice. The brisk cold had emptied the city by at least a quarter of its usual tourists. I ventured to do what any nerdy teenager at the turn of the century would have done: I went to a daytime talk show, *Sally Jessy Raphael*; ate dinner by myself at Planet Hollywood; yelled about the Backstreet Boys on MTV's *TRL* in Times Square; and saw *The Rocky Horror Show* on Broadway. My proudest moment was sneaking into a jazz club and sitting at the bar where the bartender gave me his best Robert de Niro impression. He probably realised I was underage after I fearfully ordered a Diet Coke, but he was nice. So was a cop who I chatted to for tourist tips. I remember these kindnesses because the welcoming ease at which New Yorkers made me feel was not to last. A few years later when I would revisit New York, the place felt uneasy and even hostile due to the trauma that had engulfed it after 9/11.

When Kerrin arrived we continued our fascinating journey into New York City clichés: talking to oddballs on the subway, dining at Little Italy with a guy who insisted he was Mafia, and taking the ferry to see the Statue of Liberty. In one of my photos, I stand off-centre on nearby Ellis Island with my arms up in the air as if presenting the cityscape beyond me. I wear a huge red puffer jacket, gloves and a fake Yankees beanie I bought that day. Behind me stand the two World Trade Center towers, mercilessly tall and rigid, sticking out like two columns that went out of control on a graph. I have written a message below: 'Twin Towers. Ugly but NY is cool.'

Six months later those 'ugly' buildings would be ruthlessly brought down.

—

'Ghaz, turn on your TV right now.'

'Why?'

'Just do it,' my friend tells me over the phone. It's 6.30 a.m. on a Tuesday and far too early for anyone to be calling me about something good. I quickly run downstairs and switch on the TV. A sombre newscaster repeats the one news item that dominates every television channel worldwide. Hijackers have crashed two airplanes into the Twin Towers in New York City and one into the Pentagon. It is utter chaos and the image of the second tower crumbling to rubble repeats as if on an apocalyptic loop. Terrified people below look up stunned, while covered in heavy dust and debris. My eyes are processing the images but my mind is unable to comprehend a cohesive narrative. I sprint upstairs to my parents' room. They are both getting ready for work and I switch on their small TV. That same loop of buildings on fire and people gaping halts my mum in her speech. The three of us watch, glued to our television; it's hard to look away and even harder to grasp what has actually happened.

For many of us who remember this day, the images of the second plane crashing into the South Tower, the explosion, the collapsing of both towers and the utter chaos and hysteria that ensued are branded on our memories. It is easy to remember where we were when we found out about 9/11, 2001.

'I was at home and my flatmate woke me up.'

'My mum ran into my bedroom and told me "America is under attack".'

'I went to school and the teachers didn't know what to do. So they rounded us all up in the library and made us watch the news with them.'

Like any historical event, it is shared only by a select collective. Years later when I recall this event to my tertiary students, many who were babies or toddlers at the time do not share the same photographic sense that my peers and I do. I tell them how saturated every screen was with those same harrowing images. How entrenched they are within us and our collective psyche. They do not immediately recall those shared images nor do they remember the deep impact that the event had, not only on those whose lives were directly affected, but also on the world at large. The cataclysmic event that was 9/11 unfortunately led to further catastrophes in the Middle East and beyond. I believe the canvas of the globe changed after that one horrendous day. It is as if for people of my generation, there was a normal before and a different normal after 9/11.

I do not want to diminish the pain and loss that so many people encountered as a result of these attacks. I can only speak of my own experiences, and perhaps of others, who were affected in other ways, especially as a result of the actions undertaken afterwards by the US and other superpowers.

What I do remember is the accepted racism, xenophobia and Islamophobia that grew exponentially after 9/11. I am not a practising Muslim, but culturally it is a part of who I am. In the decades after 9/11 the two became somewhat intertwined particularly in New Zealand. I say somewhat because, first and foremost, people who are Muslim definitely receive the brunt of racial abuse since that fateful day. However, the abuse does not distinguish between those who practise and those who do not. Often we are lumped into one antagonising force on the 'axis of evil'. It is similar to the type of generalised racism I encounter when overseas, based on what dominant minority I tend to look like. In the US I was seen as an illegal Mexican, while in the UK I was called a 'P**i' (the derogatory word thrown at South Asians). Oddly, after 9/11 when the Middle East as a whole became a target, the racism at least got specific:

'Terrorist!'

'Towelhead.'

'Sandn****r.'

I remember being at a birthday party on the Shore, lounging around the pool, drinking homemade cocktails, being blatantly bougie, when one of our friends in the group got vividly angry. He blurted out directly *to me*, 'Fuck Afghanistan, fuck the Middle East. We need to bomb the shit out of them!'

In my shock, I did not say anything.

But we did bomb them. The war in Afghanistan has been the longest-running war in US history, and alongside the killings, injuries and trauma, thousands were displaced and forced to seek refuge in the West. And we in the West are now vilifying those same people for wanting to flee the very wars we helped start.

I was in London in 2003 when the US and UK decided to go to war in Iraq. There was heavy opposition to this war and I attended one of the largest anti-war marches in London. Over two million people took to the streets, and for many, this was the first time they had ever done so. I had never protested in my life, believing politics to be a place full of boring men and their egos. But I believed the reasons for going to war were false and, given my experience, I was opposed to yet another war in the Middle East. I went alone but joined the millions that paraded down Oxford Street to Hyde Park. With such a large turnout, I had high hopes that perhaps those at the top would listen to us. Perhaps they'd see how angry people were and change their minds. Around ten to thirty million people protested in cities worldwide, but ultimately the protests were a failure. Within a month Iraq was invaded.

This was the era of 'Freedom Fries', hating 'Ay-Rabs' and people shouting 'Murica!' on the news. I returned to the US in 2004 to work at a theatre camp in the Catskill Mountains in New York State. I had to fill out an extra form specifically for citizens of Iran, Iraq, Syria and Libya, among others, which detailed my military training and whether or not I would declare myself a threat to the United States.

In New York, people were still suspicious and more hardened. A giant American flag was draped over the American Stock Exchange Building. Signs around the subways asked citizens to keep vigilant and to report any suspicious behaviour. Even at the Catskills, I consciously only went to the local Walmart (the only store nearby) with an American for fear of being harassed. It was a difficult time to feel at ease and overall that feeling has never subsided.

H.G. Wells' nineteenth-century novel *The War of the Worlds* revolves around the idea that Martians have invaded Earth and are attacking Britain. The Martians have enormous spacecraft that shoot 'death rays' and cause chaos throughout, until they are wiped out by earthly bacteria. It is thought that Wells based his story partly on the invasion of Tasmania by the British and how the indigenous Tasmanians were essentially nearly wiped out. I went with my parents to see the remade blockbuster movie based on the novel, directed by Steven Spielberg and starring Tom Cruise. In the scheme of fun flicks, it scored a measly 'meh' from me. As soon as we got home, however, the chaos and violence that we had seen on screen eerily reflected reality when we discovered the terrorist attacks in London.

On 7 July 2005, three bombs had detonated across the London Underground and a fourth on a double-decker bus, killing 52 people and injuring hundreds. Similar to 9/11, repetitive images of the burnt-out bus, the resultant chaos and shock circulated globally and became etched into our collective subconscious. Once again we were glued to our TV sets for hours on end. Once again we watched, trying to comprehend what had happened. For me, the attacks felt even more personal after claiming London as my third home and having left only the previous year.

It is no coincidence that the ongoing nature of 24-hour news helps embed such images into our minds. It is also worthwhile to note that the news dictates what is newsworthy based on proximity, both geographically and culturally. Terrorist attacks are almost a daily occurrence in places like Somalia, Iraq, Afghanistan and Palestine and yet our focus here remains on those places that are like ours. Western and 'peaceful'.

What became known as the 'War on Terror' ignited something in me. Like many others, I was angry about the wars, the lies, the bullshit about the weapons of mass destruction, and the destructive power of the Bush and Blair administrations. I was repelled to see the leaked images of prisoners being tortured and then ridiculed by US soldiers at Abu Ghraib and Guantanamo Bay. These images once again appalled the collective consciousness as we saw photographs of prisoners being tortured and degraded while standing next to them were smiling American soldiers giving the thumbs-up signal.

Alfonso Cuarón's 2006 film *Children of Men* (based on the novel of the same name by P.D. James) takes place in a dystopian future. Women have become infertile and humanity as a whole faces its greatest threat: extinction. As such, the world has fallen into disarray and panic. Borders are closed and migration is deemed illegal. Only Britain seems to be soldiering on. The film follows our hero Theo who must protect the first pregnant woman in decades, Kee, a refugee, and find the last remaining bastion of hope, the Human Project, which may hold the key to ensuring humanity's survival. Theo and Kee undertake a dangerous quest through Britain where we the audience see the visceral horrors of what the future could hold if such things were to occur. However, the film also invokes historical realities that *have* occurred. At train stations, 'illegals' are kept in cages, people crying to soldiers holding weapons while their belongings are thrown out of apartments into ghettos resembling similar scenes during the Holocaust. When Theo and Kee are driven through a detention centre we see a hooded figure standing on a box, with electrical wires attached to his outstretched arms imitating that of the infamous image from Abu Ghraib prison in Iraq. In the real photograph, a US soldier stands at the right of the frame looking through his own camera. He is completely uninterested in the horrific scene before him, almost shrugging it off. This image, for me, symbolises Hannah Arendt's famous theory around 'the banality of evil'. The film brilliantly depicts these horrors, often in the background of the action, which acts as a warning for what our future could become. When the migrant crisis in Europe first began in 2015, many people would refer to *Children of Men* and note its close depiction of how refugees and asylum seekers were being treated.

The 'War on Terror' and the xenophobia, Islamophobia and racism that it ignited globally, particularly in the West, made me finally lose the love I had for America. More importantly, I began to realise how anti-nationalistic I had become. In 2012, I returned to live in the US on a Fulbright scholarship to the University of Southern California. Los Angeles was the antithesis of London for me. It was vastly spread out, hard to navigate by public transport, and its famous landmarks seemed gaudy in comparison. However, I met the most wonderful people from all over the US, including New Yorkers who understood my cynicism and need to wear black every day. LA was like one giant transit lounge where people came to make their home. The people I met and loved were not the problem. They were not representative of their government. (I saw that again when I visited Israel and stayed with Israeli-born artists and activists who despised their government and acknowledged the pain of the Palestinians.)

Being a first-generation immigrant makes one think about borders, citizenship and nations. In 1993, my father,

Baby Sister and I were granted New Zealand citizenship. At the time, I didn't understand what it meant or what a big deal it could be. In fact, I was ashamed of having to attend the ceremony, as all of my friends, having been born here, were already citizens. They never had to question what it means to take on another nationality, to study and sit for a test and attend a ceremony in order to be allowed that coveted New Zealand passport. The ceremony was in a quaint community hall with the mayor of the North Shore also in attendance. Baby Sister and I seemed to be the only children there, so when an eager journalist turned up, he made a beeline for us. He wanted a photo of us with the mayor, proudly holding our important new documents. I was mortified. I did not want my secret of shame of not having been a citizen since birth to be plastered all over the news. In contrast, Baby Sister was ecstatic and with some forceful encouragement from my dad I succumbed. The photo was on the front cover of the *North Shore Times*. A colourful mid-shot of a smiling mayor and Baby Sister holding her certificate of citizenship like a prize, and me, looking mercilessly glum like I was being arrested for drug dealing. The next day at intermediate, my worst nightmare came true when one of the cool girls told me she saw my photo in the newspaper. I shrugged it off nonchalantly, 'Yeah. My dad made me do it.' And then walked off quickly before she had a chance to respond.

My mother refused to apply for citizenship when we did. She was worried that she might never be allowed to return home as it would mean giving up her Iranian passport. Technically, Iran still forbids dual citizenship, but it also requires anyone born in Iran or born to an Iranian father to hold an Iranian passport in order to enter the country. Yet the Iranian passport is not exactly the passport du jour. It is very difficult to pass through many ports holding only an Iranian passport. This paradox means that most Iranians in the diaspora will be dual citizens and the Iranian government tends to turn a blind eye to this.

After thirty-plus years of living in this country, my mother cannot imagine going back to Iran for good. When she visits Iran now she is astounded at how different it is to the home she remembers. She says that people even speak differently, using slang that did not exist back in the 1980s. The rush of so many people in the large cities takes a toll on her. She is used to the slower-paced quietness of Aotearoa. She loves spending her weekends going to the markets, sipping coffee at a beach cafe and her weeknights attending yoga and watching the locally made soap opera series *Shortland Street*.

One of the best parts of gaining New Zealand citizenship was being able to apply for a New Zealand passport. Many of us here take for granted what that tiny black book symbolises; the ease and comfort we take in passing through borders. We, as a family, learned the painful way what it means to be in possession of a less desirable book. The first vacation we took after moving to New Zealand and before gaining citizenship was to California to stay with my dad's brother in San Francisco. I remember as an eleven-year-old being utterly humiliated at LAX when we were pulled aside and our luggage was searched in front of the many other travellers; those who sped through the X-rays glancing suspiciously at us. Borders are constructs; and the more time goes on, the more borders we seem to make.

Soon, it felt that every time a group terrorised innocent people in the West, I would hold my breath and think 'Don't let it be us'. Even though it is not 'us', nor should the dichotomy of 'us' and 'them' persist, but in those moments I would lose all logical sense. I would physically feel a heavy sense of dread within. This sense of nausea is an internal anxiety and a warning of the repetitive racism and xenophobia that seems to follow such events like clockwork.

On 15 December 2014 a lone gunman took a Lindt

coffee shop in Sydney's central business district hostage. While one of the hostages was killed by the gunman, another was killed by the police shootout that ensued after a sixteen-hour standoff. The gunman was also killed. At the time, I was working for a cable television channel, alongside my father, who had been an engineer and manager at the channel since its early days in the 1990s. Our organisation was owned by a giant media corporation and so we would often rely on resources from Australia to supply our news. On this day, we were all glued to our sister channel in Australia relying on minute-by-minute details of the hostage situation. Right from the start, I felt that tense build-up within and the immediate but false hope of 'Don't be us'. The gunman was an Iranian immigrant who had gained political asylum in Australia in 1996. During the hostage standoff, he insisted the police bring him the ominous black Islamic State flag, which he demanded the hostages hold against the windows.

As every screen around us broadcast the hostage crisis in real time, we all sat in the breakroom not able to talk about anything else but what was happening on the other side of the Tasman Sea. One of our co-workers was John, a middle-aged Pākehā man. He would probably hate the fact that I use the word Pākehā to describe him, but also reacted against anything that seemed 'radically left'. John's ego, in my view, could have filled the hole in the ozone layer and today was no exception as he let loose. 'This is terrible! Why the fuck aren't we bombing them all? We should just go to the Middle East and kill them all! Fucking bomb them all to oblivion!' He kept on with this offensive vitriol so much that I physically could not stand it. Not one for confrontation, I decided to slam my lunchbox shut, huff and puff and storm off.

Later, John cornered me and earnestly pleaded that he hadn't meant offence. I was dumbfounded and angrily vented my frustration to my dad, who listened quietly.

'Aren't you angry? Aren't you offended?'

'He doesn't understand, don't worry,' he replied, making me realise the stark difference between his generation and mine. For my dad, coming to a new country, barely knowing the culture and living with the challenges was more than enough. I, and others like me, cannot imagine the fortitude and difficulties he and my mother went through in order for us to settle here. For my father it was not worth the fight to engage with one asshole.

There is the myth of the dutiful immigrant who must be grateful for having been allowed into the country and no matter what occurs they must not venture beyond that role. I wonder if that is one of the roles my dad believes he must hold. It is similar to the equally problematic myth whereby minorities such as immigrants are expected to achieve more than the average population. The myth revolves around the idea that immigrants must prove their worth for having been *given* the privilege of living here, unlike the rest of the population who do not need to question that privilege.

It is not easy to confront people and to have them listen. My mother, who is a lot more feisty and outspoken than my dad, feels this frustration whenever she has to challenge someone in New Zealand. One time she had a colleague attempt to mansplain to her the 'correct' way to pronounce Iran. There have been times where she's had to challenge people like snooty sales assistants, but my mum believes that her 'accent' (I put this in quotation marks as we obviously all have accents) allows people to belittle her. It irritates and saddens me that even within the immigrant community we are forced into a type of hierarchy based on irrelevant things like origins, skin colour and 'accents'.

Shortly after the Sydney hostage crisis, the gunman was found to have no ties to ISIS or any other terrorist organisation. He had severe mental health problems and even the conservative prime minister at the time, Tony Abbott, acknowledged that the gunman 'had a long history of violent crime, infatuation with extremism and mental instability'. Yet debate still continues on whether or not the event should count as an act of terrorism.

—

On Friday, 15 March 2019, around 1.40 p.m. local time, a lone gunman entered Al Noor Mosque and later the Linwood Islamic Centre in the city of Christchurch, and opened fire. He had strapped a camera to his chest and streamed the attack on Facebook Live for seventeen minutes, enough time for viewers to see the gunman continuously killing and wounding worshippers in both mosques before driving off to where he was finally intercepted by police. Prime Minister Jacinda Ardern later admitted that the gunman had been hoping to reach a third location, another mosque or possibly even an Islamic childcare centre.

I was in my office at the University of Auckland that day, attempting to pump out enough words to hit the word count on my PhD. My shared office is tiny and has no window. It's on the fifth floor of the Human Sciences Building. The building is an eyesore on campus. Its sterile exterior and labyrinth of beige doors and windowless cupboard-like offices inside make it feel more like a leftover Soviet relic than an inviting academic building. I don't remember how I first heard about the news from

Christchurch, but I was online attempting to find out more. A colleague, Jenny, joined me and we continually refreshed the browser to view the short online videos from news sources, each time gasping in shock. Stunned and in a daze, we didn't know how to feel. All those clichés I read in novels began to take over: I felt empty. I felt drained. I couldn't think straight. There were unverified reports of a possible bomb on the train service in Britomart, Auckland. Chaos was happening around us, but there we sat in our little bunker wondering how to process it all.

We walked over to an eatery on the usually bustling Karangahape Road. It was busy and people milled around as if it was just another day. Some were power walking home, some were sitting with friends having coffee or prosecco. I wondered what their conversations held. As more information became available, we tried to unravel what was happening in our minds. We both began to feel our little safe cocoons that we had so erroneously covered ourselves with wither away.

'But this is Aotearoa!'

'It's one of the safest places in the world!'

What happened in Christchurch was first and foremost an attack on the Muslim community. They were the targets of this terrorist attack and they have continually been the main targets of alt-right, white-supremacist groups like the one the gunman belonged to. Since 9/11, it is often Muslims who have been vilified and targeted in the media and in real life. Western news and media push an anti-Islamic rhetoric, using repetitive images of women in headscarves or burqas and bearded men praying, in stories ranging from nuclear weapons to the devastation of the war in Iraq and Afghanistan. We are constantly told to be vigilant against radicalised youth going to fight in Syria and bringing extremist ideologies back to the West. We learn about other militarised groups with extremist Islamic ideologies like Islamic State, Al-Shabab and Boko Haram. And yet what we are not consistently fed is how other extremist groups are also growing and brewing.

Germany in particular has had a huge rise in right-wing and white-supremacy groups targeting not only Muslim and the Jewish community but also refugees, asylum seekers and immigrants. The German pro-refugee MP Walter Lübcke was murdered in his own home by a member of a far-right and neo-Nazi group. British Labour MP Jo Cox was murdered by a man with far-right views. China has been ruthlessly targeting, attacking and now imprisoning Muslims in the resource-heavy Xinjiang region. The attacks on the Rohingya Muslims in Myanmar resulted in the deaths of thousands and displacement of hundreds of thousands. And now under the conservative

Modi government in India, detention centres are being built in order to house non-citizens, namely Muslims who will be the only group not allowed amnesty when new citizenship laws come into place. Even one year on, before the commemoration of the 15 March attacks in Christchurch, the now illegal video of the attacks was shared among online right-wing extremist groups who praised the gunman as a 'saint'.

I recently directed a series of short documentaries about Muslim New Zealanders for Radio New Zealand and New Zealand On Air Irirangi Te Motu. These were short profile pieces about what each person loved the most in the world: from tennis, to hiking, to the beach and cooking. Our intention was to shed a light on people from the community—that is, *our* New Zealand community who are Muslim. I did not want to focus on the dichotomy of 'them' and 'us', so consciously titled the series *This is Us*. RNZ released the first still photo from the series featuring one of the talents wearing her white veil. It's the veil she wears to pray and the title 'This is Us' is superimposed above her. Straight away, a myriad of abusive comments, ranging from Islamophobia to xenophobia to downright nasty, began popping up. The majority citing something like 'This is NOT us. This is not me!' to 'We are not a Muslim country!' to

'THIS IS certainly NOT US . . . and even on that day it still will NOT be US'. I was both depressed and angered to read such vitriol, especially leading up to the commemorations. Yes, the photograph was marketing our film and that is why it was used. But it also reflects the point of the series in that there is no them and us. We are all part of the wider community which includes people of all faiths. This is the 'us' we keep wanting to show the world. This is the 'us' we think we are and yet many of the comments showed that some people are not ready to be that 'us'.

One of the women we profiled was a young Syrian Iraqi New Zealander, activist Shaymaa Arif. In her opinion piece for *Al Jazeera* published a week after the one-year anniversary, she noted how white supremacy in New Zealand has been brewing for years, and how it has been around for centuries as the country was founded on bloodshed and colonialism. Harrowingly, she remembers how two months prior to the attacks a man in a parking lot approached her and a friend who both wore hijabs. He made the shape of a gun with his hand and mimed shooting them both in the head.

It seems as though no matter how many individuals, groups and organisations come forward and challenge extremism, every now and then we are pushed back.

———

18 March 2019, shooting in Utrecht, Netherlands.

24 March 2019, California mosque fire.

9 April 2019, bombing, Sheikh Zuweid, Egypt.

21 April 2019, Easter bombings, Sri Lanka.

27 April 2019, synagogue shooting, California.

16 June 2019, bombing, Konduga, Nigeria.

28 June 2019, bombing, Indanan, Philippines.

1 July 2019, bombing, Kabul, Afghanistan.

12 July 2019, hotel attack, Kismayo, Somalia.

28 July 2019, shooting, Gilroy Garlic Festival, California.

3 August 2019, Walmart shooting, El Paso, Texas.

10 August 2019, Bærum Mosque shooting, Norway.

20 September 2019, bombing, Karbala, Iraq.

9 October 2019, Halle synagogue shooting, Germany.

6 November 2019, shooting, Yala Province, Thailand.

29 November 2019, London Bridge attack, UK.

28 December 2019, bombing, Mogadishu, Somalia.

17 February 2020, bombing, Quetta, Pakistan.

19 February 2020, shooting, Hanau, Germany.

One of the more disturbing photographs leaked out of Abu Ghraib features a smiling US soldier holding her thumbs up next to the decaying corpse of a dead prisoner. Her gleaming white teeth contrast chillingly with the ashy purple face and open mouth of the corpse. I am reminded of Marc Antony's famous speech in Shakespeare's *Julius Caesar* where he attempts to remind the Roman citizens to focus not on the negative but on the good that Caesar did:

> *The evil that men do lives after them;*
> *The good is oft interred with their bones . . .*

I'm not sure if I am prepared to forget the evil that men do.

The
Fawn
in a
Bubble

The tiny fallow fawn lived in a bubble like everyone else in the land. She spent her days grooming her golden coat and the delicate pattern of spots that ran down her back. The fawn enjoyed living in her bubble as it was safe and secure, echoing only what was heard within the bubble. Everyone else enjoyed their bubbles too, but sometimes the fawn felt that her bubble was more of a hindrance than something good. Some days she became curious and wondered what else lay outside her bubble, but at other times she was terrified of what the others, in their bubbles, would think of her.

Every now and then, something catastrophic would happen in the world which would cause the fawn's bubble to fade little by little, exposing her to the rest of the world. At first, she was charged with excitement, but this was to be short-lived as the world did not share her excitement.

One time, a devastating conflict took hold of a region, killing and wounding millions. Some of those in their bubbles began to peep out. Years later, buildings were brought down and the world stood watching in shock. Some of those in their bubbles began to actually step out. Many years later, a monster with an eye in its chest murdered many souls. The fawn's bubble finally faded and the fawn was forced to come out. Everyone wanted to know more about this fawn and what life was like living in her bubble. The fawn was glad to let the world know, for life within a bubble was lonely. She was happy to see that so many wanted to hear her voice. She began to explain how she was like everyone else and how she desired the same things, but the world only wanted to know what it already assumed.

'Tell us about your oppressive males!'

'Tell us about your submissive females!'

'Tell us about everything that makes you different!'

The fawn tried to explain how she was like them in many ways, and how she was also an individual.

'Yes, these exist, but so does everything else.'

But the world did not want to hear what they did not already think. They only wanted to hear the echoes of their own thoughts of the fawn. They wanted only victims and sadness.

'Yes, you must have your voice heard, but only if it tells us what we want to hear.'

The fawn grew tired of this. A blanket of disappointment and frustration began to grow over her. It grew and grew and it weighed heavily down upon her until she could no longer speak. Her beautiful white spots that made her stand out faded away. The world stopped listening and went back to their own bubbles, content until the next tragedy when the questions and expectations would repeat over again.

——

Recently, I was asked to be a cultural advisor on a project that depicted Muslim Iranian New Zealanders. I was excited as I knew the writer and was very keen to advocate on their behalf. Yet when I read the piece, it angered me. It angered me because it was a mishmash of negative stereotypes and clichés about Muslims and Iranians. Oppressed mothers, abusive fathers, zealot brothers and forced marriages. It angered me more because it was written by someone who should have known better. And yet I found myself in a dilemma. All I have ever wanted is for more people from different backgrounds to be in positions to tell their stories and here is such a person, so how could I not back them? I was torn between supporting a fellow artist to gain much-needed development and criticising their work for replicating the very type of stories I hate.

When I told my concerns to the funders in charge, they merely replied with:

'I found the piece shocking and real.'

'I had no idea about these things.'

'This is a story we need in New Zealand right now.'

Needless to say, the project was selected.

Another time, I attended a theatre production run by a theatre company that is prestigious, but is not widely considered to support diverse voices, nor have them in their audience. I was excited because a Middle Eastern friend was getting the chance to play a Middle Eastern role, one which was an integral part of the narrative. I sat with a large group of friends, and friends of friends, ready for the play. I had never felt so physically drained with anger as I had that night. My friend, as excellent as she was, was one of only two actors of colour on the stage (and in the whole production, which was written and directed by Pākehā men). Her role was reduced to another negative stereotype of a victimised Middle Eastern woman in a veil, wandering war-torn deserts. Once the play finished, I was ready to vent with my fellow theatregoers, but was stunned to learn how invested they were in the production:

'I found the piece shocking and real.'

'I had no idea about these things.'

'This is a story we need in New Zealand right now.'

My anger quickly subsided into contemplation. Was I just the wrong demographic? Is projecting a story full of stereotypes still better than no story? I grappled with this dilemma for a while and come back to it even today.

As a writer and artist, I have tried not to rely on clichés and stereotypes, which is very difficult. It is easy to copy what has been done before and know that it will succeed *because* it already has. It is much harder to find something that is authentic and challenges what is already known. This is not to say that I haven't made mistakes or used negative stereotypes in my own work, but hopefully I've learned from my mistakes. Surely it is the role of the artist to challenge what is already out there, not simply to replicate it.

This is part of the burden of representation we face as artists of colour; the burden that minority artists must only write about their marginality, their ethnic identity, and that their story is representative of everyone within that ethnic group. The privilege of white characters (and artists) is that they can represent anyone and everyone in humanity. In his famous chapter 'The Matter of Whiteness', cultural theorist Richard Dyer writes: 'The claim to power is the claim to speak for the commonality of humanity. Raced people can't do that—they can only speak for their race. But non-raced people can, for they do not represent the interests of a race.' Perhaps the story my friend had written has a place in the world as do clichés and stereotypes, but when they are the only stories being told it becomes toxic.

———

One boring Sunday evening, I put up a screenshot of American actress Sally Field from one of her earlier Hollywood films on my Instagram story, captioning it, 'I hate you, Sally Field.' Immediately I received messages from other Iranians telling me how much they despised this movie when they first saw it. This film incited so much rage from Iranians abroad that when I told a renowned fellow writer how much Iranians hated Sally Field as a result, he encouraged me to write a play about it.

The film *Not Without My Daughter* (1991) is based on the memoir of American woman Betty Mahmoody who married an Iranian doctor, Sayyed Bozorg 'Moody' Mahmoody. While living in Michigan in 1984, Moody convinces Betty to return to Iran for a short visit. Hesitant but devoted to her husband, Betty agrees, and along with their young daughter Mahtob, they travel to Tehran in the midst of a war and regime change. Moody's family is highly traditional and religious and through their encouragement Moody decides to stay in Iran, despite Betty's desire to leave. Moody becomes possessive and violent, using the newly established regime as support for his role as the patriarch. Betty becomes imprisoned in a place that is fanatical, violent and, in her own words, 'primitive and backwards'. Soon Betty finds a brother and sister who help people like her escape and the film follows Betty and Mahtob's harrowing illegal journey through the deserts to Turkey and finally back home to America.

I was only a child, but the film enraged me so much that I've refused to read the original source. As a thriller, the film provides excitement and rush amidst cheesy, upbeat music cues. The acting is decent from the leads, including the English-American actor Alfred Molina playing Moody (I am not even going to argue about the classic whitewashing here), who manages to speak acceptable Farsi throughout.

Not Without My Daughter at least attempts a sense of verisimilitude in its depiction of 1984 Tehran, packed with murals of Khomeini, new Islamic flags (that replaced the monarchy flag), dirt roads, Paykan cars and masses of women in chadors. As can be expected from American cinema at this time, Iranians are shown as the fanatical Other. They are seen arguing and yelling at Betty, often in

Farsi that is not subtitled (this will once again be replicated in Ben Affleck's *Argo* decades later). Betty as our conduit is always attacked and never seems to get a step right. When a Komiteh sister jumps out of a truck and rushes to Betty with her rifle yelling at her to pull her hijab tight, a surprised Betty cries, 'A little bit of hair just fell out, what's the big deal?'

Betty, supposedly like the viewer, is the ignorant but innocent tourist accidentally thrown into the chaos of a much more archaic, seemingly lawless, savage land. Alongside depicting Iranians as uncivilised barbarians, the film also has a blatant evangelical agenda of promoting the good Christian over the evil Muslim.

Throughout the film, the Iranians are intertwined with a Muslim force that needs to be put in its place. Betty suddenly becomes a devout Christian, wearing her crucifix necklace and spending her nights praying to Christ with Mahtob, with secret hopes of returning home by Christmas. Moody continually yells about how he is a pious Muslim and how Mahtob must be brought up in a Muslim country in order to become Muslim, and he even sends Betty to Koran classes. The film ends with Betty walking through empty Turkish streets before hearing the fluttering of a giant US flag beckoning from its high perch at a US embassy, practically reaching its golden hand out to her before finishing on a rather misguided epilogue: 'Many women are held against their will in foreign countries.'

My friend Romy tells me how she was made to watch this film in her theology class at a strict Catholic high school in Auckland as it was an 'accurate' representation of the Islamic faith.

Hollywood films in the 1980s are known for their blatant patriotism in some respect due to the conservative Reagan administration with its pro-military stance. *Not Without My Daughter* was released in 1991, a decade after the hostage crisis, but still in the midst of anti-Iranian sentiment. The film capitalised on this and infused it with an Islamophobia that seems never to have vanished. *Not Without My Daughter* is not alone in its one-dimensional representation of Iranians and Muslims, but it is one that Iranians abroad will always remember, because it was probably their first introduction to how they were being represented on screen. In fact, at one point when Molina was heading to a rehearsal for a different project in London, he was approached by an Iranian who asked if he was the actor who played Moody. When Molina replied 'Yes', the man punched him in the face.

I once had a conversation with a fellow actor about constantly being put up for clichéd roles. I complained about the devout Muslim and 'victim' roles I would be offered, while he vented about constantly being cast as a member of Hitler Youth due to his blond hair and pale complexion. One of my favourite industry moments comes from the time I was cast in a commercial for a global communications company. My role was as newscaster for an international news show and the whole point was to be an ethnically vague team. At the wardrobe test I walked out wearing a full Indian sari. My 'co-anchor', a Parisian bloke originally from Senegal, came out wearing a fez and long woollen cloth draped over his shoulder, making him look like an extra from *Casablanca*. We both rolled our eyes the full 180. That look represented everything we felt about this façade. In that tiny moment, he and I epitomised everything that is wrong with how people of colour are marginalised on screen. We were merely dolls, decorated by well-meaning but ignorant people who lumped us into generic boxes of which they knew nothing and, worse still, refused to learn anything about. If there had been just one person of colour in that department or within the heads of production, they might have had the insight to suggest something different. But there wasn't.

In the last few years, the media industry has been throwing around words like 'diversity' so much that it has now become a buzzword, a trend: a word without meaning as in 'eco-friendly', 'millennials' or 'a Trump leadership'.

Diversity in media has become about hitting targets and quotas to satisfy superficial goals rather than addressing real needs. What is needed is representation. Many people speak out about the need for representation and for good reason. British-Pakistani actor and musician Riz Ahmed claims that representation is fundamental to culture. Every time someone sees themselves reflected on screen, it means they are 'part of the national story' and that they matter, are valued and feel represented. To do this, we need to be represented in positions of power. It is about being in the boardrooms and in the decision-making forums. It is not enough merely to see a person of colour on screen; they need to be creating the screen in the first place. Representation is everything.

Love
in the
Time of
Corona

Italy

I look in a hand mirror and straighten my fragile, red paper beak. I adjust my blue culotte and velvet waistcoat; a shoddy costume made on a tight budget. I look to Lou who stands in her frilly nightgown worn over jeans, putting on her white bonnet. She continues to glare at Henry, the posh boy with puffy red cheeks and floppy brown hair that makes him look like a loveable Disney character. Henry not only snores loudly in his sleep, but talks too. Last night he shouted something about Winston Churchill. Lou dislikes him intensely.

'I'll sing with you from behind the curtain, alright?' he whispers, his Etonian accent marked by an incessant lisp.

I nod, terrified, and step out in front of our makeshift velvet curtain.

An enormous hall is full to the brim with seated, well-dressed adults, each staring at me, standing on the stage in my cheap velvet and paper nose. Henry starts to sing and like a vaudeville victim, I join in, absolutely mortified at having to sing in front of such a large crowd. I have a terrible singing voice. Like many children at primary school, I was as ignorant of this as I was of staying in tune. My ignorance aided my pride in being an active member of the choir. I still remember singing biblical classics mixed with Cliff Richard bangers. In high school, an earnest drama teacher once wrote on my audition application, 'Cannot sing at all'. So it is with twisted irony that I am chosen to be the lead in this ridiculous rendition of *Pinocchio*. We begin:

'Hello! Hello! I am Pinocchio!'

I wave my arms around and jump attempting to overshadow my pathetic vocals with my average dance moves. This absurd puppetry is part of a theatre tour around Italian schools; it's a way to encourage students to learn English. The organisation hires fresh-faced acting or teaching graduates in the UK, and pays them to travel the breadth of Italy in groups of three. The three are packed into a dingy station wagon and are expected to perform well-known fairy tales in English to various groups of Italian school children. One day I am *Cappuccetto Rosso/* Little Red Riding Hood who gets chased by the evil wolf/Henry through hordes of primary school children screaming at the top of their lungs '*Lupo!*'/'Wolf!' Other days I am doing skits with Lou while attempting to add our own witticisms alongside the structured basic scripts we have memorised. Today, I am little Pinocchio, the wooden doll who gives away his balloons in order to become a real boy.

Throughout my tragic charade, I suddenly lock eyes with a man a few rows back. He has the most perfect symmetrical features of any human face out there, his head of blond curls having been meticulously placed on his head. He looks like a painting, probably Dorian Gray before his surrender to temptation. In fact he looks like a young Jude Law playing Dorian Gray. He smiles and his teeth almost glimmer. The crowd stays rigidly emotionless as my voice trembles in the silence. Dorian Jude continues to smile. I fake cry about losing my balloons. Later we have to meet Dorian Jude as he is a big player in children's book publishing. He continues to smile at me but my insecurities about singing and dancing stop me from engaging with the most beautiful man in the world.

—

Aotearoa/New Zealand

'Gym selfie!'

A woman yells as others around her holler in delight. A couple of women fall into hysterics as they yell between their exasperated laughs, 'Gym selfie!' The women frantically attempt to find 'gym selfie' on their makeshift bingo boards and cross it out. The taskmaster in charge of this chaos continues by clicking on her computer screen as another male face pops up. He has a cheeky smile and some questionable facial hair as he looks directly at his waiting audience. The taskmaster scrolls through and stops on another photo of presumably the same guy, this time a tiny figure on a mountaintop overlooking Machu Picchu. The taskmaster practically screams, 'Finding self! Who has "finding self"?'

The women in the room once again fall into a deranged gaggle of laughs and screams, each furiously attempting to find 'finding self' on their Bingo board. Welcome to Tinder Bingo. The task is to find the usual, common and overused tropes on a user's profile photos. Amidst the fun, the taskmaster can still choose to swipe 'yes' on any potential suitors. That is, after all, the overall aim of the entire game.

My friend Stacey and I created our own version of Tinder Bingo after drinking far too many merlots and realising how terrible many straight men were at advertising themselves. We grew wary of the badly lit selfies taken in run-down Holdens, and felt so accosted by the half-naked torsos that left nothing to be desired, that we came up with our own entertainment. After all, these apps are not just for finding dates. They are games—and as singles everywhere know, dating is just another game.

'I hate women who put profile photos of themselves drinking beer on Tinder. It's so unfeminine. I don't find it attractive at all.' Kieran is a tall bloke in his late thirties with short dark hair that sticks to his head like a GI Joe doll. He has some excellent freckles and is a genuinely good-looking guy. It's a pity about his personality. We are having a chat in the tiny back garden of a renovated villa in upmarket Ponsonby. I finally decide that a sneaky ciggy is not worth the lecture about what kind of woman dickhead Kieran finds attractive, so I go back inside.

Looking around, the party is in full swing as various strangers stand talking to each other as their eyes wander around the room in an attempt to find a more attractive person. Everyone is in their thirties and forties, professional and probably living in equally hipster flats with mid-century vintage decor and obscure lights. They are also single and this is a singles party started by my friend Emma. Much like her namesake in Jane Austen's novel, Emma wants to help lowly singles, such as myself, find mates. The rules are simple: only singles are invited and each single must bring another single of a different sex (it's a very heteronormative binary kind of party). They are then let loose.

It's an interesting foray into the modern dating world that no reality show could ever capture. Nearly every guest suddenly finds their inner Casanova and confidently approaches strangers. It is unlike the usual parties where Kiwis often stick to their own groups, terrified of even acknowledging the presence of others. At the beginning everyone is polite and somewhat shy, jugging down their alcohol to help converse with actual strangers. Soon it becomes obvious that everyone has a mission, ranging from finding a potential mate for life or a mate for the night to ignoring any mating whatsoever and enjoying the booze and snacks. Some girls become instant allies, helping their friend target the one lone boy who seems to be the Brad Pitt in a sea of pitiful Brads. They force their friend forward and create a protective shield around her, stopping other women from entering the perimeter. Generally speaking, after attending a few of these parties, I notice that it is women who are making the most effort. Most men seem to just hang around oblivious to the strategic manoeuvres operating around them. Aggressive women? Kieran would hate it.

I enjoyed coming out of my comfort zone and chatting to complete strangers who willingly came to such an affair. I never found a mate, having spent one ill-fated party with an ex, and the first party befriending Emma, but they were fun excuses to meet people who also knew the hardships of being single in a world that forever seems to be geared towards couples, and in a world where online dating has become the new normal.

'Online' and 'dating' are two words that can incite fear and dread in almost any person who was old enough to remember the days where 'dating' in New Zealand constituted downing RTDs in a parking lot and pashing some skateboarder in the corner of a makeshift dance floor at a local rave. Dating was not something that you undertook, dating was something that just happened to you.

—

Ian 38, Engineer

English flag emoji

Swipe right for some good banter.

In a strange and terrifying move, Ian decides to call me before any potential meet-up. Anyone who thinks it is normal to call a stranger on the phone is obviously not from this century. Ian has an astonishingly hoarse voice with a very thick northern accent. He sounds like a seventy-year-old miner. His confidence soon shifts into cocky when he says, 'You look like you enjoy sex.'

I was not aware of this.

The first official dating app for straight folk was Tinder, created by friends, Iranian-Americans Sean Rad and Justin Mateen, in Southern California. It began as an app for 'rich and affluent' college students, particularly those in the Greek system, which for anyone who has watched an American teen-sex comedy seems to be a trashy country club for privileged bros and gals. I'm sure that is not true for all fraternities and sororities but after living only a street away from USC's frat row, I can say the generalisations are not far off. In its first year, Tinder claims to have been making twelve million matches a day and is now worth billions.

It is an odd feeling to go on an online dating app for the first time. You are both curious and fearful, having your photo out there deeming yourself single. For being single means having a stigma attached and no matter how many loved-up couples tell you it's not that great, and no matter how many independent happy singles chide you for being sucked into societal ideologies, it is still a hostile world to singles. Singledom articles are aplenty giving us contrasting views:

'The hidden, horrifying costs of being single.'

'7 reasons why being single is awesome!'

'Help! I'm single and lonely!'

'14 benefits of being single.'

British actress Emma Watson calls it 'self-partnered', which had critics commenting that it was solely because she just couldn't 'get blokes'. Comedies like *Fleabag* praise the heroine going it alone. Numerous books about being single and how to either stay that way or change it for the better are always on the self-help shelves. It seems as though women must be disliked for wanting a relationship but also scorned for not wanting one. As with anything women-related, everyone has an opinion on how we should live, whether you want that opinion or not. There are boxes to be filled in where your relationship status becomes as important as your name. Facebook, first created for privileged and cool college students as a way to meet and date, also centred on users' relationship statuses.

Filling in boxes has been a bigger burden in my life than I wish to admit. Whether it is ticking the correct relationship status or ethnicity, it has always created mild panic within me. I once had a twenty-minute argument with a surveyor at the Museum of London who refused to tick the box 'Asian'. At another time I was rather amused when I told an Auckland University administrator to tick the box 'Middle Eastern', to which she innocently asked, 'Is that near Fiji?'

My Aunt Mina had a slew of boyfriends in high school back in Iran. Popular, stylish and always up for fun, she was one of five sisters, so needing to make herself stand out became a daily goal. Mina has remained single for her entire life and become one of the most independent people I know. Sadly, Mina has a lifelong illness and sometimes needs to seek help from the family and medics. She has been admitted into hospital more times than I can remember, and seeing her sadness every time she has to spend more than a night there makes me realise how much many of us take our good health for granted. I can see how much it pains Mina to have to rely on others when she has been so fiercely independent for nearly 70 years.

Mina is the nicest person I have ever met, always putting others first. When she first moved to Aotearoa she became a sort of surrogate grandmother for us, albeit a young and stylish one. While she was living with us, settling in and finding work, she would babysit Baby Sister and me, and the cousins. It would be Mina who did the school runs, holding our hands as we crossed busy Auckland roads and taking us to the movies on the bus.

When I got older, Mina would tell me to find someone, to not try and do it all alone as she had done, for even though she was happy, the world is not made for singles. 'You feel like half an adult.'

Mina would tell me that whenever we'd go on family holidays, while the married folk got to share rooms and share costs, Mina would have to share with one of the children. Mina's dream was to visit Europe. She had once gone to East Germany when it was East Germany. She met a friend who lived on the West side and together they ventured to the border in Berlin with her friend's husband. The young German guard flirted with Mina and her friend and so granted them a three-day visitor's visa but refused to give her friend's husband entry. A photo of Mina, snug in a trendy peacoat and standing in the middle of a half-empty GDR plaza, hangs in her living room today. At one time, she had collected a bunch of travel brochures from the local agency, folding the edges on the pages of tours she wanted to do: London, Milan, Rome, Prague and Paris. Due to her waning health, Mina couldn't take long-haul flights, so she threw out the brochures.

'You feel like half an adult,' she would repeat.

It was Plato who once said that human beings were all born with four arms, four legs and two heads until Zeus cruelly parted us. Zeus believed that people would lose their strength and would stop being wicked if left on their own two feet. So, now we must spend our entire lives finding our other halves in order to become complete humans.

—

Chad, 32, Director

i like travelling

'Best date ever!' New York Times

'A real charmer' Dalai Lama

'****' My mum

About a drink in, Chad tells me how he grew up in a very strict Christian household and later became a missionary in the US. About two drinks in, he argues with me about the transatlantic slave trade, believing that 'African people' were to blame for the whole 'debacle'. Drunk with anger, I leave and he later texts asking if we could meet again. I politely reply with the universally used 'I don't think we're a match' and he comes back with a detailed 300-word text about how I was wrong and how he can offer things I wouldn't be able to refuse. I refuse.

There are different stages when first testing online dating. The first being the superficiality factor that everyone needs to get over, and they seemingly do, after the first go. It's an odd feeling to be looking at a never-ending factory line of photos of strangers and an even stranger feeling to realise your own issues around what you find attractive. These apps, unlike traditional dating sites, do not require much in terms of a profile, relying first and foremost on photos. The game is simple: you swipe yes on someone and if they swipe yes on you, you match and can chat via text. This process in itself feels like chat roulette where getting a match incites a rush of dopamine, not unlike winning a bet; a bright yellow starburst erupts on screen aligning your profile pic with that of your match. It's exciting and thrilling. Until the person stops chatting to you. Some people are so settled with texting that they become terrified of meeting up in person. What grown adult wants a pen pal? Some people prefer daytime coffee dates, which I find preposterous. If I am meeting perfect strangers, I need alcohol and poorly lit corners that accentuate my good side.

Sometimes, they or you don't look anything like the image they/you have in mind, and so comes the look of disappointment. I've both shown that look and seen it played out. It's a pretty devastating look that can really gnaw at your self-confidence. Sometimes the date goes really well and you spend four or five hours pounding back drinks and laughing about nonsensical things, often the dreaded online dating experience. Other times, it's boring as hell and you're glad you only ever have dates during weeknights for fear of losing your weekend to some dropkick who loves quoting *Family Guy*. I've found love on these apps. I've found heartache. I've found everything in between, but for me, these apps have given me something that I failed to have when younger. An actual dating life.

—

Tim, 39, works in government

Music, surfing, wine, great chats.

The night before I met Tim, I realised that years ago, he used to date a good friend of mine from high school. One day he told her to stop dressing like a child and they broke up. In retrospect, this should have been enough for me to have cancelled at the last minute, but I naively believe people have the capacity for change after fifteen years. We met after work at an overpriced pub in Britomart. Tim has no sense of humour. He doesn't even smile. Neither of us contacted each other again.

Everything in the world today, including dating, needs to be immediate. Like laboratory mice, we are conditioned to want immediate satisfaction. We like the superficial things, judge the most minute details and swipe left or right with such ease, we forget the things that exist below the surface.

'I don't like how he can't differentiate between "you're" and "your".'

'He's put "school of hard knocks" as his education.'

'That's a terrible shirt.'

Or has this been dating all along? I spent my twenties with depression, crushing any hope for romantic liaisons, though there were crushes aplenty. Dating for me only took off in my thirties, which is actually an embarrassing confession because by then you are supposed to be super-sexual and have relationships (or be virginal and ready for marriage).

When younger, Baby Sister and I would always cringe every time someone even kissed on screen, as our dad would quickly reach for the remote control to change the channel. One of the community 'uncles' was so strict that he would forbid his daughters from watching even the most sexless shows like *The X-Files*. Even today, my dad will leave the room if a sex scene is forthcoming. If a boy ever did call our house I would sprint to the phone, for fear of my folks answering. In hindsight, I don't think my parents would have cared. Rules become mixed when you grow up in two cultures that often collide. Sometimes you have to push the boundaries just to know what the boundaries are.

Nowadays, with no grandchildren in sight from either Baby Sister or me, my dad has loosened up. Every Sunday I make a point to visit the folks and to indulge in my mother's excellent Persian cooking. I know every person believes their mum or dad to be the best cook, but I have it on good authority from the community of aunties and uncles that my mum is a brilliant chef. On one freezing Sunday in June, I complain to my folks about how cold my room in my flat is. My dad argues that the temperature's not that bad yet. I say that's because there are two of them in the bed. Without a beat, my dad drops this zinger, 'Well maybe you should find someone to be in your bed so you're not so damn cold.'

Dad: 1, sad daughter: 0.

—

People's Republic of China

A river of people flow in and out of the Forbidden City entry gates. Our group waits for something we know not. A group of Chinese high-school students grab two of our group, an animator from the Czech Republic and a filmmaker from Finland. They take group photos with them as if they are famous celebrities, their blonde hair practically gleaming in the light against the group of dark brown. The school kids giggle and thank them. Our group is then led into the city by our tour guides, a few students from Beijing Film Academy where we have all been staying as part of an international student film festival. It's a place filled with people but somehow there is no chaos. People move into the palace grounds in an orderly and calm way, taking photos, looking at the supreme architecture of the dynasties that ruled China throughout the centuries. It is the largest imperial palace in the world and often hosts around 80,000 visitors a day. That number must be legit as the sea of people seems endless, most of them visiting Chinese from other cities, towns and provinces. They are also the tourists who love taking photos of foreign tourists, me included. There were plenty of times in my visit where a kind woman would tap me on the arm and mime a clicking photograph with her hand. We would stand side by side, arms around each other like old friends and take a photo. It was rather amusing to know that you were almost as fascinating to look at as the Great Wall of China.

The Forbidden Palace is impressive due to its enormous size and historical legacy. The palace grounds surround a large lake, which at the time we visited was hosting a giant floating rubber duck created by a Dutch artist. Oddly, the buildings are empty except for the masses of people that walk through. It was an odd contrast to see such barren structures invaded by so many people and yet still feel a sense of emptiness. It reminded me of visiting the imperial palaces (or what was left of them) with Ellie in Tehran. One of the most famous was Golestan Palace, where the giant Marble Throne was the centrepiece of coronations of kings until Reza Shah in 1925. Every inch of the palace was covered in jewels and mirrors; it was as if we were entering the inside of a gold disco ball. The walls and ceilings glittered proudly while the actual space was completely empty. There was no furniture, no props or anything that suggested that human beings once inhabited it. During and after the revolution these palaces (along with many wealthy homes) were looted. Now attempting to salvage what they can, the palaces gain a bit of income from visiting tourists desperate to see some architecture that is not a mosque.

I wander around the Forbidden City with Daniel, a filmmaker from Germany who was born in East Berlin in the early 1980s to a Russian-German mother. Daniel has a hipster beard and speaks perfect English with a slight lisp. We bond over a cigarette. Daniel loves to talk; he is a storyteller and has a great way of remembering moments from his life and recounting them with excitement. Soon we fall away from the group and find ourselves strolling through the Forbidden City like two lovers reciting existentialist philosophies as they do in the *Before Sunrise* trilogy. Naturally, we both love those films. We smoke our Double Happy cigarettes from red packets and reach the top of a hill just outside the city walls. This spot offers an excellent view of the entire palace grounds. The palace looks like a movie set with thousands of extras roaming around, waiting in groups to be told where to walk next. Everything seems spotless as there are many lone cleaners picking up litter left by the tourists. For a city of over 21 million people, Beijing is eerily clean. At the lookout, Daniel points to four CCTV cameras on one pole eying every direction possible.

'This country is full of cameras, have you noticed that?'

We continue our wandering, discussing films, writing, travel, fears and love as if we had been friends for an eternity. We walk past the Forbidden City gates as an enormous painting of Chairman Mao looks down on us. We talk about what we love in Beijing and what we find odd. He tells me about life and growing up in the GDR. I tell him what I remember about Iran. We smoke two whole packets even though we both insist that we have given up. Sitting on a curb near the bus stop, we wait for our tour group. It is quite an amazing feeling to meet someone who lives on the other side of the world but with whom you have so much in common. After an hour of waiting, we finally realise that the tour group must have left without us and that we were likely waiting in the wrong spot. We continue to walk and talk all the way back to the film school.

Daniel and I stayed in touch over the years as he continued his nomadic life visiting other countries to either hike or undertake artists' residencies. I started my PhD. One year he told me he was coming to New Zealand to experience our world-famous hiking trails—none of which I had ever seen. I'm not a hiker nor remotely interested in anything outdoorsy like many of my Kiwi mates. My parents were big urbanites, growing up in apartments, visiting beach villas when they went to the Caspian Sea in Iran or the Coromandel in New Zealand. We didn't camp or hike or even own a decent sleeping bag. In later years, my dad has suddenly grown an appetite for the great outdoors and often goes on expeditions with his mates from his football teams, all of them Iranian. One time I had to help him buy supplies for their trek across the Tongariro Crossing. My dad was shocked to see how expensive a good sleeping bag was. 'Isn't it just a blanket?' he asked before shrugging his shoulders and purchasing it anyway.

When I picked up Daniel from the airport, we were

both ecstatic to see each other again. He was super
excited to have finally made it. Shuffling his backpack and
breathing in deeply, he cried, 'Even the air is different
here! Can't you sense it?'

'Not really,' I smile.

Daniel stayed at my flat for a few nights before heading
to the South Island. I felt like there was definitely something
between the two of us, but neither of us were very good
at admitting it. My German friend Jenny blamed it on
Daniel being German; she believed that her people do not
know how to flirt.

Halfway through the following week I received a
message from Daniel. He had stepped on a tent spike
which pierced his foot and now had thrombosis. He
needed to come back to Auckland. We spent the next two
weeks together, him in agonising pain, me cleaning and
cooking for him, which was frustrating for both of us. If
there is one thing that can kill romance, it is thrombosis
in the leg. We were both miserable by the time he returned
to Germany. We stayed in touch for a while until he found
someone else. I will always have this one regret: the great
German lover that was not to be and the stupid bloody
tent spike that ruined it all.

—

Adam, 38, Software Engineer

Dying for a drink after the apocalypse is over.

Rhys, 35, Construction

Let's have our first date on a socially isolated picnic.
We can share sanitiser and wine.

Roopesh, 40, Entrepreneur

Looking for a bubble buddy. Lockdown chat?

—

The first detected cases of an unknown virus occurred in the city of Wuhan, China on the eve of the new decade. Countries all over the world closed their borders in a panic. On 11 March, the World Health Organization declared Covid-19 a pandemic. Within only 100 days, the novel coronavirus had spread worldwide. On 2 April, the global infection rate of Covid-19 passed the one million mark with 50,000 people dead. Various countries went into strict lockdowns. On 8 April, Wuhan's lockdown ended after 77 days. By 18 May, global recorded cases passed 4.8 million with 300,000 deaths; New Zealand came out of full lockdown on 27 April and moved to Level 1 (the lowest alert level) on 8 June. At the time of writing it's hard to know how it will end.

—

I used to watch pornographic films for a living. It's a great opening sentence, especially on a first date. When I worked at a cable television network, one of my roles was overseeing various channels as they played to air. Three were adult channels that played XX and XXX pornography twenty-four hours a day, seven days a week. As someone who did not grow up with online porn, it was an eye-opening insight into such a world.

The first time I watched an adult film was with my friend Yoong. We were too embarrassed to go to the video store ourselves so waited outside as her older sister went in. Later, the three of us watched it on Yoong's VCR. About twenty minutes in, both Yoong and I got bored and instead went online to chat with random strangers. The internet was not yet at peak porn; this irony was lost on us.

It's not surprising that the porn we broadcast was for straight men. We even had guidelines on what was outright prohibited (male on male but not female on female) and what was 'frowned upon' (any pornography that subtly suggested violence or paedophilia). That last one was obviously troublesome and even when the network hired a censor, films still slipped through the radar, and it was up to us to spot them, become disgusted/disturbed/horrified and report them.

Most of the time the porn was generic and boring. As a writer, I found the repetitive stories so terrible that I couldn't tell if that offended me more than the actual porn. Some were actually funny, almost mocking the viewer, such as porn with mimes that involved no sound or parodies of films that utilised obscure prosthetics. But many ventured beyond the fine line of acceptable entertainment to the violence, misogyny, racism and blatant objectification that porn is notorious for. At its core, porn is visceral, offering no subtlety or layers of depth. It requires only a physical response; there is no emotion. The empty apathy that porn triggered in me had to be challenged with something else. I ended up watching a lot of cheesy Disney shows and One Direction pop videos instead. I wanted something hopeful, pretty and clean.

It may sound trite coming from someone in a privileged position like myself, but that same need for hope resurged during the war on coronavirus. As Aotearoa went into lockdown in March, my days were spent glued to the news cycle, absorbing the alarming statistics, and in the evenings I watched dystopian films. The air felt unsettled and unnerving and many of us were on edge, terrified of the unknown. And yet, it felt as though people were closer to each other than before, as we all shared a common bond. I found it fascinating to browse through the same dating apps as before. In isolation, the loneliness is obviously more amplified. Apparently, during the pandemic, there was a surge in new online dating apps. People still want to connect even if it means meeting on a video chat. Tinder even made a few of its usual paid options free, including a free-for-all to 'swipe' on anyone in the world. The intention to find someone is still there, even in the midst of a terrifying human catastrophe. Perhaps there does exist something deeper than smiling photos of men finding themselves on Machu Picchu.

The
King
and I

'Go to the end of Regent Street and take a left; it's not far,' I tell the confused but thankful Spanish tourist who sighs, relieved, then runs off with her group of friends, loudly yelling at them. She probably knew the directions, but her group failed to listen and believed a true Londoner would know. I, a 'true Londoner', was waiting on the curb for my friend Samira and as the minutes became hours, I pondered my sanity and friendship. It is not uncommon for Persians to be late. Many make being late an art form; it's part of their incessant need to challenge the Gods of Time. Once in Iran, I was waiting in the car for my cousin Ellie and after running back to see where she was, I found her in the midst of a full-body self-tan, after confidently telling me she'd be a 'mere five minutes'.

Another eager tourist asks me for directions, as yet

another lines up behind him. I have become an accidental information kiosk. I call Samira back angrily. 'I'm a mere five minutes away!' she cries back, her high-pitched tone almost singing. Samira is always high on energy and never one to dwell on the darkness of life. An hour later, we head into the club Chinawhites, a posh celebrity-obsessed nightclub, hidden below the stairs of a nondescript door and sandwiched between some high-street shops and McDonald's Piccadilly.

The club is ridiculously over the top with everything I loathe about clubs today: VIP corners, an abundance of tight white pants and glitter tops, and severely overpriced weak vodka. We love it. Samira is my cousin through marriage, who also moved to Auckland from Iran at a young age, but unlike me, her confidence was never shattered and her personality radiates energy, which oozes from her curvy frame. Samira, like many other Persian women, has perfected her preening and grooming to such an exact science that never a hair is out of place, even when she's downing a bottle of vodka while dancing on a table at 4 a.m. on a Tuesday. With Samira, it's dead easy to get into places that forbid mere plebs. We practically saunter into the VIP section with other friends including a fellow Kiwi Persian, Golnaz. Inside we are surrounded by beautiful women who all rock the same unamused look of ennui on their perfectly sculpted faces. Apparently VIPs should not act like they're having fun; only sad plebs do that. One of the statuesque goddesses, reclining on her seat, tells me how excited she is that the drummer of an average rock band is there. Her sullen face barely flickers so I am unsure as to whether she is excited or not. Reclining goddess then points to a corner where an overtly tattooed short dude stands, looking terrified about the insane number of primped females around him.

'And Prince William and Harry are also here,' she says, nonchalantly.

For some terrible reason, Yoong and I used to be near obsessed with the royals during high school. It was partly sarcastic, more as a way to get through Tudor–Stuart history classes while annoying our loveable teacher Mrs Atkinson with inexcusably excruciating questions like, 'So, if the wife-killing misogynist lived in Hampton Court Palace, where do the royals live now?'

'I think I'd look good getting married in Westminster Abbey, Miss.'

And Mrs Atkinson, always in on the joke, would reply with full shade, 'You'll never even get to meet a royal, Ghazaleh, let alone marry one.'

The joke became my own personal legacy after I inscribed this statement in my final yearbook, 'My aim in life is to marry Prince William—or at least shake his hand.'

So it is with this fated legacy that Samira and I head out to find the royals, my own sword in the stone.

The VIP section is heaving. People are now dancing to terrible pop songs famous in the early noughts, while drinking shots and becoming rowdier and louder. The room is no bigger than a typical modest lounge, with strategically placed lights. Two slim bouncers stand at the entrance, each wearing a designer suit. They look as bored as the goddesses lounging on the sofas. I dance with Golnaz as we scope out the room. After all, that is the sole purpose of being in a club. A few bald-headed middle-aged men are scattered throughout, wearing sweaters and khakis. They are not talking to anyone except themselves. These are royal bodyguards. Unlike other celebrity security who are often ginormous Vikings who stand out like terrifying beacons, these bodyguards are small and unnoticeable. They stalk the room with such awareness that it is obvious they could probably kill with just one swift flick of their thumb. I strike up a conversation and feel like I'm chatting to my dad's friends. It reminds me of the time Prime Minister Jenny Shipley visited our high school and instead of being in awe at chatting to the leader of our country, my friends and I swarmed around her bodyguards and asked them a multitude of questions. They, for their part, absolutely loved it. Shipley, probably not so much.

Suddenly I spot Samira, entangled in a tight group, her blonde highlights flashing as loudly as her smile. Her arm waves frantically beckoning me to come over. I make my way through the crowds, the energy tense, as is any room where people are attempting to show their faux disinterest in the famous.

When I reach Samira, she grabs my arm and practically shouts, 'Ghazaleh, meet Prince William, and Prince William, this is my friend Ghazaleh. Oh and she's totally in love with you!'

Cue a moment of tense silence; this is what great movie scenes are made of. Wills, tall and good-looking before his hair retreated in later years, smiles and replies, 'I'm just his lookalike.'

We chat a bit more before the flow of bodies begins to dominate and overpower the group, so much so that my bodyguard mates step in and make everyone disband. The plebs and VIPS are parted once again.

Later, without knowing how or why, Golnaz would end up pashing with one of Prince Harry's closest friends, while Harry sat alone watching the party-going plebs, his dark cap guarding his VIP status from unsuspecting eyes. I stole his hat at one point, but we never chatted. In a surprising twist, the bloke Golnaz was with ended up giving her Harry's mobile number, and so Golnaz took it upon herself to call that number days on end. A week later, upset that the bloke never called her, she benevolently concocted this story: 'The palace called me and apologised for not responding to me. They were really nice about it.'

It seems that Golnaz was no stranger to mingling with the rich and powerful, as later we found ourselves at an MP's house party, where an older, hefty gentleman took a shine to me. I found his conversations about his million-pound business as dull and brutish as his face. I realised Golnaz and I would never become friends when she asked me, 'Why don't you want to date him? He's rich and he'll buy you things like Cartier jewels.'

We stopped hanging out and in years to come I would learn that she was having an affair with an Arab sheik and was so convinced he would leave his wife for her that she went to a fortune teller to learn about casting spells and other magic.

Iranians in the diaspora can be extremely cunning when they want, and I often wonder as to the origins of this trait. For many, stretching the truth comes naturally, as does outright lying. It also makes us more suspicious of others, which is not a trait I would attribute to many New Zealanders, who are often more open and trusting.

There is no doubt that there exists a strong historic and cultural reason behind this Iranian characteristic, not least influenced by past trauma, but this lies outside of my scope here. Azadeh Moaveni, a second-generation Iranian born in Palo Alto, California lived and worked as a journalist in Iran in the early 2000s where she learned a great deal about her own Iranian identity. In her self-reflective memoir *Lipstick Jihad*, she notes this culture of deceit that Iranians seem to excel in when she quotes a friend who tells her, 'You'll find that lies are natural for people here. Having a façade is normal, because being honest is such a hassle.'

The hassle being the constant oppression and torment from the state or society in general. With generations of Iranians brought up in a culture where truths must be hidden away from prying, corrupt eyes, it is vital to not be so trusting. Azar Nafisi in her well-known memoir *Reading Lolita in Tehran* also notes this idea of lying becoming practically second nature to Iranians living under oppressive regimes. It becomes of utter importance to not tell the truth to the Shah's SAVAK police or the Islamic Republic's Basij force. Secrecy becomes a vital tool in keeping one's private pleasures distant from those who are continually trying to intercept and invade them.

London became a playground where I felt free to undertake whatever experiences I wanted. My mother, a worrier ridden with anxiety, was a strict matriarch and so, for me, never learning how to make my own decisions affected my decision-making as an adult. Later I realised that these insecurities seemed a natural fit for my mother, who in her late twenties, with a baby and toddler in tow, moved to a new country with a culture and society so foreign to her that she didn't know how she could trust it. It is difficult to understand these complexities when you're young, as really, all you want is to be like everyone else. However, it was also because of this need that I became a curious adventurer, albeit a cliché, thinking that in order to become an adult—even more importantly to become a bona fide artist—I would need to experience everything I could, no matter how ludicrous, unhinged or dangerous. This behaviour could also be due, partly, to a nomadic streak; being displaced at such a young age puts one continually in a state of motion. I was trying to find out not only where my home was, but also who I was and what I wanted in life. And so it was that by the age of thirty, I'd had no fewer than thirty jobs, some lasting only hours, but all coming from a place of intense intrigue and a need to find my place.

X-Ray Filer

Apart from a two-week paper route, this was my first official job. My mum was furious that a thirteen-year-old would want to start working, and she cried, 'You have your whole life to work! Why would you want to start now?'

For me, it was not the actual work. It was the opportunity to have a different experience; in this case it meant filing X-rays and documents for the radiology department at the local hospital for two hours a week. I got the job through a friend and together we would spend the first hour reading about a stranger's ailments and broken bones, sometimes becoming spooked when said stranger had the words 'deceased' printed across their file. The second hour, we would flip through the shared library and pick up the heftiest Mills & Boon romance novel and sift through the pages to find the raunchiest, sexiest scenes and read them out loud to each other, often roaring with laughter or expressing disgust afterwards. The job was easy, but dull, and I remember thinking how absolutely miserable I'd be if I had to work there full-time. The snob in me always felt that I would achieve great things and that these experiences were merely tiny steps towards a grandiose career in something I had a passion for. Nothing was good enough, and it was this misguided tenacity that gripped me for years. This restlessness, I later learned, is an obvious companion to feeling rootless and displaced. The grass *must* be greener on the other side, it must be, because I've ventured to it!

Waitress

I thoroughly believed that in order to become an artist— that is, one who is tortured, talented and addicted to vice—one had to experience everything in life: the highs and lows, the beautiful and ugly with all the risks involved. So it was with much glee and secret excitement that I got a job at a club in Ealing, London. I was far too reserved to be a dancer so waitressing seemed the best option. After all, all the great writers wrote what they observed and there was something thrilling and sexy about working somewhere so risqué. How wrong I was. Strip clubs are just another example of the horrors of capitalism, devoid of meaning and overtly sexist, racist and downright unhealthy for everyone involved. More unsettling was that I was unprepared for the incredible faux displays of power that such a place required. While the women who worked there had my back, entrenching a strong sense of sisterhood, the men acted as though they could be the worst versions of themselves. It was a sad insight into a sexist world that often exists in everyday life, except here it was on display loudly, blatantly and without shame or opposition. It was also hard physical work, waitressing through the small hours of the night. I have no idea how the dancers did it. They were almost robotic in their strength. It was a weird world and after just one night, I never returned.

In contrast, I also waitressed at a bar and club in central Soho that welcomed gay men. It was aptly named Sanctuary. Despite some exquisitely brilliant clichés such as a woman in a red sequined dress singing piano tunes every Monday, and beautiful men wearing designer winter coats, the clientele were much friendlier and less abusive.

Usher

For a film nerd, this job was a dream come true, and for someone shy and not used to having more than a handful of friends, few of them male, it was a great introduction to a wider social circle, including boys. I was forced to wear a comical uniform that consisted of a sparkly blue waistcoat and matching bow tie. The theatre, meanwhile, was like its own university dorm, complete with drunken shenanigans and even criminal behaviour. Once I walked into the box-office cubicle only to be confronted by all the staff lying on their fronts, their hands behind their heads in surrender. An armed burglar had just robbed them and had made a dash for it. The trauma was short-lived, however, and for most of the time we dealt with ignorant customers (a personal favourite was raiding pre-teen hooligans getting secretly drunk in the theatres) and each other's love lives. At the time, I believed the perfect way to flirt with a boy was to shove into him at a rave, where he, being under the influence of a copious amount of drugs and alcohol, would have no choice but to go with it. I was not mature for my age.

In London, another favourite gig—for they are always gigs, working contract to contract, often odd hours of the day and night, never having weekends—was being an usher at a West End theatre. This particular establishment had the popular musical *Chicago* on every night and twice on a Sunday. By the third week I knew all the lyrics and dance moves by heart. The job was easy, the crew excellent, mainly consisting of young actors, dancers and other theatre hopefuls each working this job to sustain their audition hustle during the day. Again the myriad of customer abuse did not diminish and we were often confronted with London's finest: drunken hens, couples shagging in toilets and wannabe celebrities demanding superior service.

Customer service jobs are plentiful for young, artistic hopefuls needing to pay rent and for nights out. The work is easy to pick up, relies on shiftwork and offers a plethora of other like-minded young folk providing endless social arrangements. I loved it. But I hated the customers. It is through customer service that we truly see some of the terrors of humanity. Rudeness, anger, desperation and frustration are common, but the one that reigns supreme is the class disparity and snobbery. The hierarchy that exists is crudely shown as many people treat those in the service industry with such disdain that it took a global pandemic for many to realise just how essential and important customer service roles were. This disparity was amplified to an extreme when I worked at a large charity event.

This annual event is run by a well-known mogul who is a heavy hitter in the entertainment game.

I am in charge of two tables of guests: politicians, a couple of well-known movie stars and even the London mayor (and now UK prime minister) Boris Johnson. Boris stays glued to his paperwork, clearly a workaholic even at such a flashy event. The giant screens around us suddenly begin playing a short promotional video begging people to donate money to 'poor Romanian orphans'. Our job is to encourage the rich guests to donate as much money as possible to this supposedly noble cause. There is no other information about the cause, or what it will do. Just sad, crying Romanian children. At one point the mogul shouts at us ushers to 'get more fucking money!' from the punters.

Looking around, I feel like I am in a terribly over-the-top Hollywood movie, like *Titanic*. Working-class waiters bustle around constantly, clearing tables, hastily bringing drinks. The rich folks at their table care not, so entrenched are they in their own conversations and so blatantly above it all. Even within the tables there exists a class hierarchy, for the wealthiest people sit in the tables right down the middle, the exact spot where the mogul manoeuvres his large frame throughout like a zeppelin, dropping down to an unsuspecting guest every now and then with his crude smile coaxing more money out of them. And yet, we ushers, food staff, waiters, security and drivers run around, working for minimum wage in order for these people to give money to a charity that most likely does not even exist. If ever there was a time to hit an iceberg, I had wished that night was it. Alas, it was not to be. Shoved in a taxi with five other ushers, we are later driven home.

Temp

Being a temporary office worker feels fitting for someone as nomadic and unsettled as I. The contracts are short and the work varies as much as the locations. One week I was called into an anti-terror think-tank organisation that needed me to move around some email contacts. They expected this job to take four days. It took me four hours, and so for the remaining days of the contract, I would follow up numerous emails—mostly to students at universities in Pakistan who had enlisted to help the organisation fight extremist propaganda and enlistment by terrorist groups. Our boss himself had been a former member of a well-known extremist terror group until he renounced it and turned his life around; he now runs meetings, panels and this organisation to combat extremist terrorism.

It was a surreal place to work considering I was just a temp. The small central office was crowded with other workers as a giant television screen above played BBC News non-stop. The man who made me sign my life away was a former MI6 spy. I later learned that despite their insistence that the organisation was independent, they were heavily funded by the UK government.

It was both heartwarming and heartbreaking to have students email me back, determined to help battle extremist ideologies that were constantly invading their campus. Their eagerness and passion was so authentic that it made me realise that this situation was serious, and beyond my skills and experience. I had to ask, what am I doing here?

Often I feel as though I do not belong, whether it is in the place I am living or in the industry I am working in. This imposter syndrome is quite common apparently for people in the arts, and particularly women. It's as if deep down, our pesky superegos are peeking out and demanding attention. 'This is above you. You are not good enough!'

It took me years of therapy to figure this out, and even now, I find myself retreating to it, like some overbearing dark entity within. I wonder if it is also a result of being an immigrant child, forever wondering where your place is in the world, and worried if you are worthy of the sacrifices your parents made in giving you a 'better life'.

Barista

Some of the worst customers I ever had the displeasure of serving were coffee addicts; they were stressed and desperate for their caffeine hit, and verbal abuse and downright nasty behaviours were quite common. A favourite story involves one disgruntled giant who, time and time again, would yell at me that *he* had taken the wrong drink; in retaliation, and knowing that this was a con he was playing around all the coffee chains, we snuck some cleaning fluid into his drink alongside some other unmentionables and watched with glee as he sucked it all down. Do not fuck with people who serve you food and drink; it just makes common sense.

Setting aside this global chain's infamous disregard for any kind of human or environmental rights, working there provided me with things I had been looking for when growing up. I found a sense of belonging within the community of tight-knit friends I made there, and I also felt that I had finally begun 'living' like everyone else. I did not feel like an outright outcast, nor did I feel complacent, still giving my opinion, which sometimes contrasted with those of my colleagues.

My colleagues and I were all of a similar age, in our late teens and early twenties, thrown out into the world after high school, trying to figure out what it was all about. Although there were some disparities in class and background, in this place and in these years we were all connected by a shared sense of emerging adulthood. One of the first good friends I made there was Brad: a quiet Pākehā bloke with an old soul that earned him his nickname, Old Man Brad, who much like me had grown up in a middle-class sheltered bubble of close friends. It was through him that my social group grew and soon we were all hanging out at the coffee shop, late after closing, having parties and deciding which love triangle to get involved in. I was forced to watch All Blacks matches and go camping for New Year's. It sounds banal and odd to reminisce about this basic-level *Melrose Place*, but for me the ordinary held something extraordinary.

Perhaps because without my consent, I felt marginalised from the beginning, I spent years taking back that non-choice and consciously stepping outside the box. That streak never really faded, but I also grew to accept the mainstream. I still refuse to enjoy rugby, but I love attending a pub quiz. I still dislike camping, but after thirty years of living in Aotearoa, I have finally travelled to the South Island and embraced its epic beauty. Aotearoa has grown on me because I have accepted my place within it, as an Iranian–New Zealander, an expat, an immigrant; as a woman; as an artist.

Maybe, for me, it was a bit like *The Wizard of Oz* after all. After so many years thinking my fortunes and prospects lay elsewhere, in the US, London or even Iran, I realised, much like Dorothy, they were here all along. I just needed to take that damn yellow brick road, meeting scarecrows and men without hearts, to fully understand it.

Belonging is a constructed idea that is changing and forever evolving. Living in a diaspora is much the same. It is often fraught with exilic memories or nostalgia for a forgotten or faded homeland, but it is also a place where the new can be exciting, challenging and positive. My journey is not uncommon—not just for others who have grown up in similar circumstances, but also for most people in general, growing up and finding their place.

One of the most prominent cultural theorists from the twentieth century, the late Edward Said, aptly titled his memoir *Out of Place* (1999). Said was born in Palestine and lived in Lebanon and Egypt before moving to the US where he completed his degrees, including a PhD from Harvard University in 1964. As such, Said felt like an outcast in nearly every school, particularly due to his identity as an Arab-American. *Out of Place* focuses on an in-between place, and the marginalisation Said felt allowed him a different and more empathetic perspective on the world; even a positive one. In another work, Said notes:

> *Most people are principally aware of one culture, one setting, one home; exiles are aware of at least two, and this plurality of vision gives rise to an awareness of simultaneous dimensions, an awareness that—to borrow a phrase from music—is contrapuntal.*

In so much of the work written by exiles and those spread around the world, there is a constant longing and need to find a home or a place that accepts them. Often it becomes a binary position or the person is stuck in a type of in-between limbo, neither here nor there. I'm starting to believe that I have more than one place and that I do not have to solely align my identity with just my Iranian or my Kiwi side. I am privileged in that I have found home in more than one place and that I consider my identity to be made up of being a hyphenated Iranian–New Zealander amidst many other elements. For me, writing these essays has been an attempt to make sense of it and, as Said terms it, to think and write 'contrapuntally'. I hope to encourage others to do the same.

Further Reading

Where Rockets Fall and Pōhutukawa Grow

Amanolahi, Sekandar, 'A Note on Ethnicity and Ethnic Groups in Iran', *Iran & the Caucasus*, vol. 9, no. 1, 2005, pp. 37–41, available online at <jstor.org/stable/4030904>.

Axworthy, Michael, *Revolutionary Iran: A history of the Islamic Republic*, London, UK: Allen Lane, 2013.

Black, Ian, 'Iran and Iraq Remember War that Cost More than a Million Lives', *The Guardian*, 23 September 2010, available online at <theguardian.com/world/2010/sep/23/iran-iraq-war-anniversary>.

Lu, Rose, *All Who Live on Islands*, Wellington, NZ: Victoria University Press, 2019.

Malek, Amy, 'Memoir as Iranian Exile Cultural Production: A case study of Marjane Satrapi's *Persepolis* series', *Iranian Studies*, vol. 39, no. 3, 2006, pp. 353–380, available online at <tandfonline.com/doi/abs/10.1080/00210860600808201>.

Peterson, Mark Allen, 'From Jinn to Genies: Intertextuality, media, and the making of global folklore', in *Folklore/ Cinema: Popular film as vernacular culture*, edited by Sharon R. Sherman and Mikel J. Koven, Logan, Utah, USA: University Press of Colorado, 2007, pp. 93–112, available online at <jstor.org/stable/j.ctt4cgnbm>.

Brown Girl in the Ring

Dalton, Harlon, 'Failing to See', in *White Privilege: Essential readings on the other side of racism*, edited by Paula S. Rothenberg, 5th edn, New York, USA: Worth Publishers, 2016, pp. 15–19.

Flood, Alison, 'How the Sweet Valley girls grew up', *The Guardian*, 30 August 2012, available online at <theguardian.com/books/2012/aug/30/sweet-valley-francine-pascal-interview>.

The Girl from Revolution Road

Brodsky, Judith and Ferris Olin, *The Fertile Crescent: Gender, art, and society*, New Brunswick, USA: Rutgers University Institute for Women and Art, 2012.

Ceasefire Centre for Civilian Rights, Centre for Supporters of Human Rights and Minority Rights Group International, 'Beyond the Veil: Discrimination against women in Iran', report published 16 September 2019, available online at <minorityrights.org/publications/beyond-the-veil-discrimination-against-women-in-iran-english-and-persian>.

Golbakhsh, Ghazaleh, 'Monsters, Slackers, Lovers: Exploring cultural identity in Iranian diasporic cinema 2007–2017', PhD thesis, Auckland, NZ: University of Auckland, 2020.

Satherley, Dan, 'Jacinda Ardern graces the world's tallest building, the Burj Khalifa', *Newshub*, 23 March 2019, available online at <newshub.co.nz/home/new-zealand/2019/03/jacinda-ardern-graces-the-world-s-tallest-building-the-burj-khalifa.html>.

Shirazi, Faegheh, *The Veil Unveiled: The hijab in modern culture*, Gainesville, USA: University Press of Florida, 2001.

War of Terror

Arif, Shaymaa, 'Centuries of white supremacism to blame for Christchurch shooting', *Al Jazeera*, 16 March 2020, available online at <aljazeera.com/indepth/opinion/centuries-white-supremacism-blame-christchurch-shooting-200315093919706.html>.

BBC News, 'Sydney siege: Gunman had "history of violent crime" says PM Abbott', *BBC News*, 15 December 2014, available online at <bbc.com/news/av/world-australia-30489552/sydney-siege-gunman-had-history-of-violent-crime-says-pm-abbott>.

Wired.com, 'Disturbing New Photos From Abu Ghraib', *Wired.com*, 28 March 2008, available online at <wired.com/2008/03/gallery-abu-ghraib> (viewer discretion advised).

The Fawn in a Bubble

Dyer, Richard, 'The Matter of Whiteness', in *White Privilege: Essential readings on the other side of racism*, edited by Paula S. Rothenberg, 2nd edn, New York, USA: Worth Publishers, 2005, pp. 9–14.

Ellis-Peterson, Hannah, 'Riz Ahmed warns lack of diversity on TV will drive young to Isis', *The Guardian*, 2 March 2017, available online at <theguardian.com/culture/2017/mar/02/riz-ahmed-warns-lack-of-diversity-on-tv-will-drive-young-to-isis>.

Love in the Time of Corona

Grigoriadis, Vanessa, 'Inside Tinder's hookup factory: How the dating app changed the way single people get together', *Rolling Stone*, 27 October 2014, available online at <rollingstone.com/culture/culture-news/inside-tinders-hookup-factory-180635>.

Safi, Michael, '100 days that changed the world', *The Guardian*, 8 April 2020, available online at <theguardian.com/world/ng-interactive/2020/apr/08/coronavirus-100-days-that-changed-the-world>.

The King and I

Moaveni, Azadeh, *Lipstick Jihad: A memoir of growing up Iranian in America and American in Iran*, New York, USA: Public Affairs, 2005.

Nafisi, Azar, *Reading Lolita in Tehran: A memoir in books*, London, UK: Fourth Estate, 2004.

Said, Edward, *Reflections on Exile: And other literary and cultural essays*, London, UK: Granta, 2013.

Acknowledgements

I t has been an absolute privilege to be afforded such a platform, and a dream come true to become a published author. Many people are not given such opportunities, so I want to thank a number of people for making this happen.

I should also note that some names have been changed in these essays, as many of my family members are very private individuals. In saying that, I want to acknowledge their real names here.

Mahnoosh, Jamshid and Galareh for your uncondi-tional love. Your admiration for literature and the arts never wanes.

Shahin, Mahshid, Shahyar, Sahand, Hamoon, Nazee, Mo and Nick for your support throughout the years in Aotearoa.

The wider whānau of aunts, uncles, cousins and

grandparents in Iran, Aotearoa and across the diaspora.

My amazing friends who lent me their stories, and also those who did not fit into these narratives—maybe the next book!

The wonderful Jenny Hellen for pretty much everything: taking a chance on me and supporting my voice. And the rest of the brilliant team at Allen & Unwin, including Leanne McGregor, Leonie Freeman and Erena Shingade, as well as freelance designer Megan van Staden.

Editor Barbara Larson for her hard work and for teaching me what 'house style' is!

Copyright Licensing New Zealand and the New Zealand Society of Authors for awarding me a 2020 CLNZ/NZSA research grant, which helped me immensely.

My supervisors, Dr Stephen Turner and Dr Shuchi Kothari, who worked tirelessly on my PhD, a document that provided the basis for some of the historical content in this book.

Galareh, Carly and Yoong for reading the early drafts and assuring me they weren't totally shit.

My flatmates, Chelsea, Rhys, Tim and Gus, for keeping me sane while I wrote this book during a worldwide pandemic lockdown.

AUTHOR PHOTOGRAPH BY SACHA STEJKO

About the Author

Ghazaleh Golbakhsh is an Iranian–New Zealand writer, filmmaker and Fulbright scholar. Her writing has appeared in a range of publications, including *The Spinoff* and *Villainesse*. She studied screenwriting at the University of Southern California before completing a PhD in media and communications at the University of Auckland.

Ghazaleh has made various award-winning short films, including the documentary *This is Us* for RNZ/NZ On Air, and is developing her first feature-length screenplay in 2020.